FIRST FOLDS

✳ IN THIS FIRST SECTION YOU WILL BE SHOWN HOW TO MAKE SOME EASY BUT PRACTICAL AND USEFUL OBJECTS: A STATIONERY FOLDER AND VARIOUS KINDS OF 'FOLDELOPE' – A VERY CLEVER KIND OF ALL-IN-ONE LETTER AND ENVELOPE – AND TWO TYPES OF PICTURE FRAME. ✳ YOU WILL ALSO LEARN TO FOLD THE FLAPPING BIRD, A PERENNIAL ORIGAMI FAVOURITE.

✳ YOU WILL FIND ALL THE PROJECTS IN THIS SECTION SIMPLE TO DO ONCE YOU HAVE MASTERED THE BASIC FOLDS. ✳

DOCUMENT FOLDER

This is the simplest project in the book and would be the ideal starting point for a newcomer to

origami.   The folder is complete in only five easy-to-follow steps.

Because the model involves only a few folds,

you can use a good thick paper or thin

card which will make your folder

much more hard-wearing.

If your paper is very thick,

you can score the folds

first to make folding

easier. Start with

a sheet of paper

measuring

45 x 62.5 cm

(17 ³/4 x 24 ³/4in) to make this

practical and versatile folder.

INSTRUCTIONS FOR DOCUMENT FOLDER

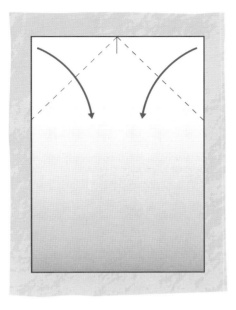

1 Mark the centre of the top edge of the sheet, then valley fold the two corners in to meet in the centre.

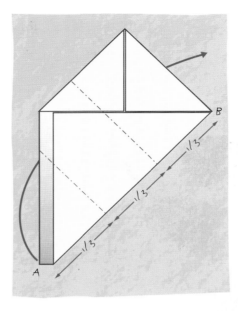

3 Measure the length of the diagonal edge from A to B and divide into thirds. Make parallel peak folds at these points.

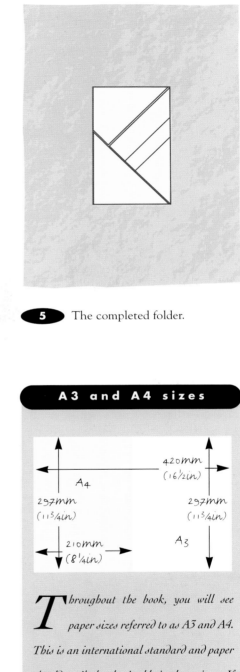

5 The completed folder.

A3 and A4 sizes

*T*hroughout the book, you will see paper sizes referred to as A3 and A4. This is an international standard and paper should easily be obtainable in these sizes. If you are unable to obtain it, the relevant measurements are given above.

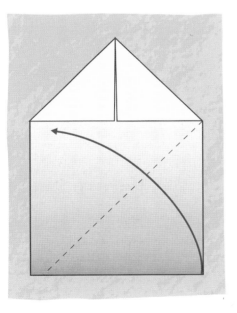

2 Now valley fold the lower right-hand edge up to meet the base line of the triangular section.

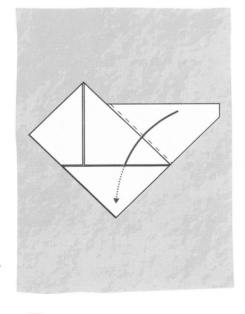

4 Unfold the flap that lies between the back and front of the folder, then valley fold it in the direction of the arrow and insert it so it tucks into the front pocket as shown.

FOLDELOPE *Mu*

One of the most practical uses to which origami can be put is shown in the next three projects. A 'foldelope' is essentially an all-in-one letter and envelope – you write your letter on one side of a sheet of paper, then fold it so that the writing is contained inside the envelope that you create. Here we show three different designs which are as easy as they are attractive.

You can have fun decorating your finished foldelope; a few of our suggestions can be found on the following pages. We have named our three foldelopes Mu, Sa *and* Shi *in honour of Musashi, a famous 16th century Japanese swordsman, strategist and artist.*

This Foldelope is the most decorative of the three designs as it is folded to appear as if it has a band wrapped around it. This is, in fact, a locking device formed by fitting the top part of the 'band' over the lower part. This movement is simplicity itself once you get the hang of it! Start with a sheet of paper measuring 210 x 297 mm (8 1/4 x 11 3/4 in.)

INSTRUCTIONS FOR FOLDELOPE MU

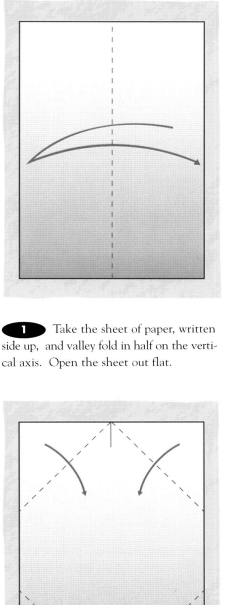

1 Take the sheet of paper, written side up, and valley fold in half on the vertical axis. Open the sheet out flat.

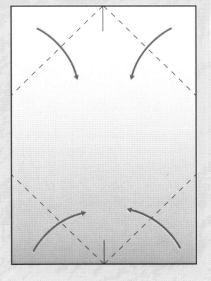

2 Valley fold each corner in to the middle of the sheet.

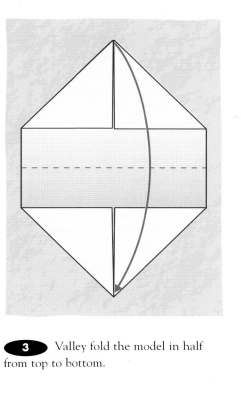

3 Valley fold the model in half from top to bottom.

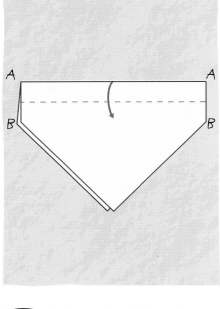

4 Make a valley fold by taking point A to point B as shown.

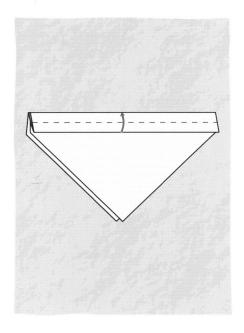

5 Take the bottom of this flap and valley fold it in half in an upwards direction.

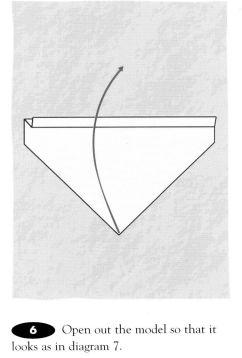

6 Open out the model so that it looks as in diagram 7.

INSTRUCTIONS FOR FOLDELOPE MU

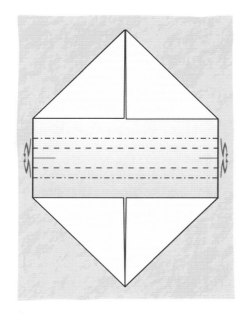

7 Now use the folds you have created to make a pleat as shown in the next diagram. The top part of the pleat will fall naturally into place, but the two lower folds need to be redefined to make the lowermost fold a peak fold and the one above a valley fold.

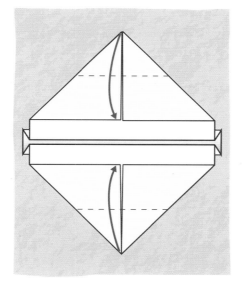

8 Valley fold the top and bottom points of the model to the bottom edges of the triangles as shown.

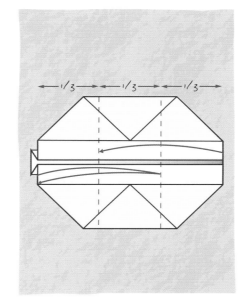

9 Divide the model into approximate thirds by making vertical valley folds. Unfold the left-hand flap, keeping the right-hand flap in place.

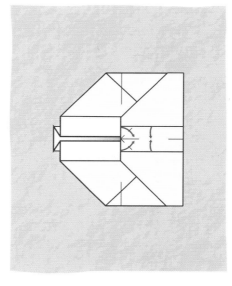

10 Make the band in the centre of the right-hand flap taper to a point by folding in the two diagonal valley folds shown. Now pinch the two sides of this band together.

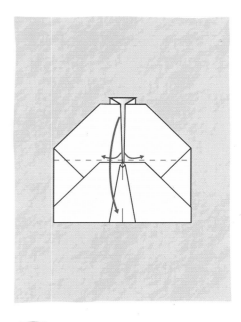

11 Hold the pointed band, still pinching the sides together, and insert it into the band on the upper flap by gently sliding or tucking the top band onto the lower one. This movement will bring the top flap down over the lower one, so that it makes the valley fold shown.

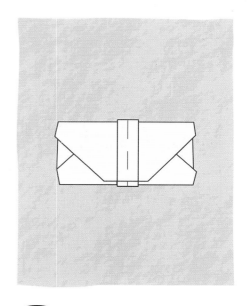

12 The foldelope is now complete. Write the address on the reverse side.

This attractive design features decorative 'cut-off' corners, and would be perfect to use for invitations. A natural textured paper like the one shown here would make an unusual and stunning wedding or christening invitation.

You can experiment with decorations for your foldelopes too: to recreate the ones shown here, simply

FOLDELOPE *Sa*

raid your sewing box for suitable odds and ends or buy ready-made tassels and ribbon from a haberdashers or notions counter. You can buy ready-made seals but we made our own, using a kit bought in a craft shop. The seals you produce will probably not be as perfectly round as the shop-bought variety, but this makes them all the more appealing. As with the other foldelopes, you should start the project with a sheet of A4-sized paper (210 x 297 mm/8 $^{1}/_{4}$ x 11 $^{3}/_{4}$ in).

INSTRUCTIONS FOR FOLDELOPE SA

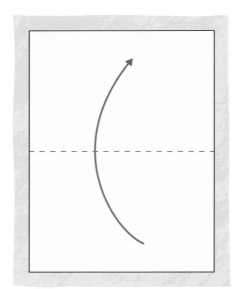

1 With written side down, valley fold the letter in half from bottom to top.

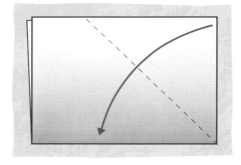

2 Valley fold the top right corner of the top sheet down to the bottom edge.

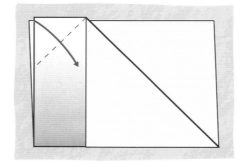

3 Valley fold the top left corner in to meet the vertical edge of the triangle.

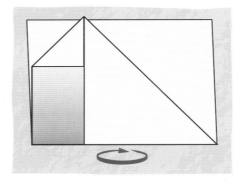

4 This is how the model should look. Now turn it over ...

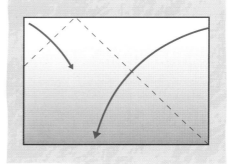

5 ... and repeat steps 2 and 3 on the other side.

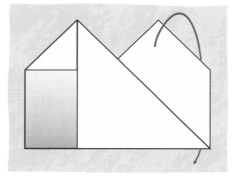

6 Unfold the back sheet in the direction of the arrow to create the shape shown in diagram 7.

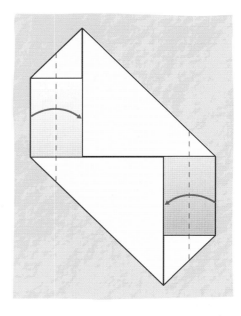

7 Valley fold the left and right vertical edges of the model to meet the vertical raw edges.

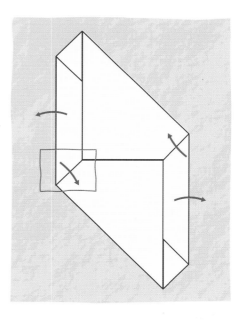

8 Lift the left-hand panel formed in step 7 and untuck the concealed triangular flap of paper underneath it (just below the horizontal crease running across the model). Close the panel again, bringing the concealed flap from the inside to the outside and folding it down to form a square pocket (see diagram 8a). Repeat on the right-hand side, this time forming a pocket just above the horizontal crease.

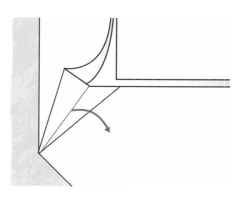

8a This is a close-up view of how the concealed flap is untucked and folded down on the outside of the model.

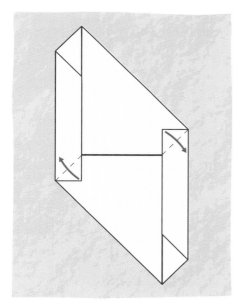

9 Now valley fold the corners of the square pockets in the direction of the arrows, thus forming triangular pockets.

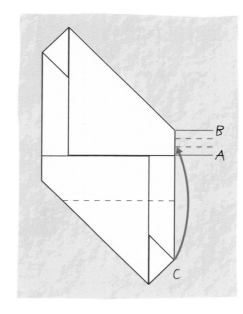

10 Valley fold the lower section of the model up in the direction of the arrow so that point C sits one third of the way up from A to B.

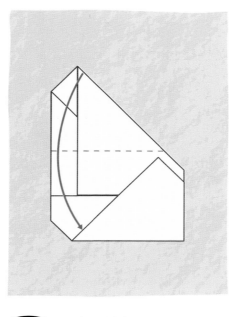

11 Valley fold the upper section down so that the diagonal edge lines up with the diagonal edge of the flap formed in the previous step.

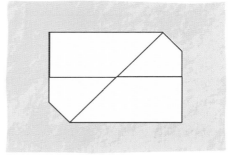

12 Open out flap formed in step 11 ...

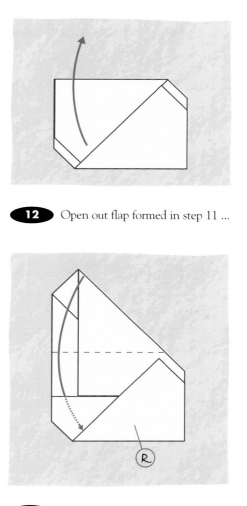

13 ... then re-fold it, this time inserting the point into the triangular pocket. Repeat steps 11-13 on the other side, inserting the point into its respective pocket.

14 The completed foldelope *Sa*. Write the address on the reverse.

FOLDELOPE *Shi*

This foldelope design is the most conventional of the three and produces a standard envelope shape. Start with a sheet of standard writing paper.

If you prefer not to write directly on to your chosen paper, you can write your letter on thin paper and place it on top of the foldelope paper. Fold the two sheets as if they were one; the result will be a letter contained within the foldelope.

Once you have mastered the technique, you can be creative with your choice of papers, matching the pattern of the paper to the purpose of your letter. Do bear in mind that you should be able to write on the paper – if you choose a particularly knobbly or absorbent paper it would be a good idea to test it first.

INSTRUCTIONS FOR FOLDELOPE SHI

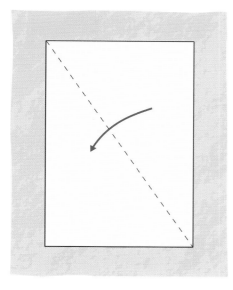

1 Turn your letter over so that it lies blank side up. Valley fold in the direction of the arrow, forming a crease from top left to bottom right corner.

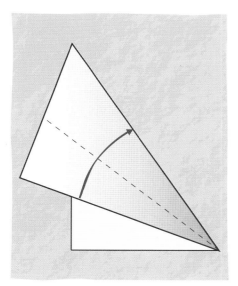

2 Valley fold the bottom edge of the top sheet up to meet the top edge.

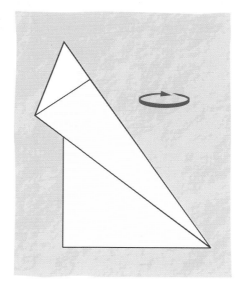

3 The model should look like this. Now turn it over.

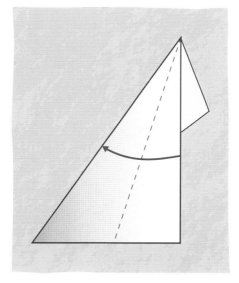

4 Valley fold the right-hand edge of the top sheet across to the left edge.

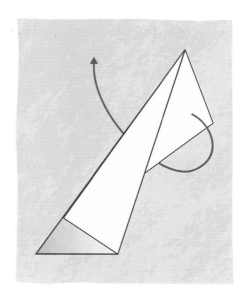

5 Unfold the back sheet in the direction of the arrow to form the shape shown in diagram 6.

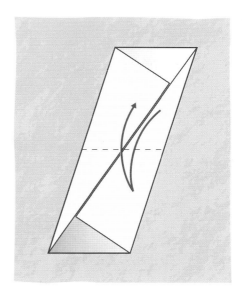

6 Valley fold the model in half from bottom to top. Do this by first rolling the bottom edge over and aligning it with the top edge, slightly overlapping, so that the two form a continuous line running at exactly the same angle. Then press flat firmly and unfold.

INSTRUCTIONS FOR FOLDELOPE SHI

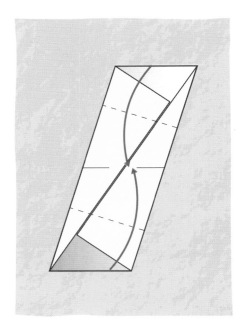

7 Keeping the side edges of the model aligned, valley fold in the top and bottom edges so they butt together at the centre in a diagonal line. Refer to step 8 to see how the model should look.

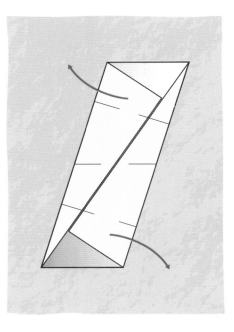

9 Open out the remaining two folds in the direction of the arrows...

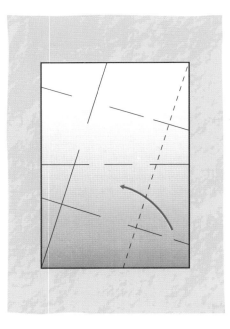

11 Now refold the existing valley fold-line on the right ...

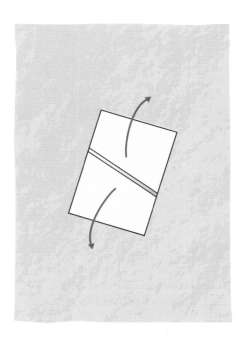

8 Now open out the folds that were formed in step 7.

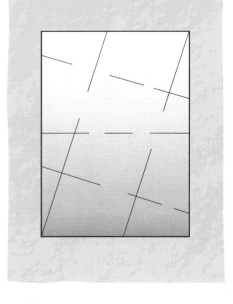

10 ... so that the letter is now fully opened out with written-side facing.

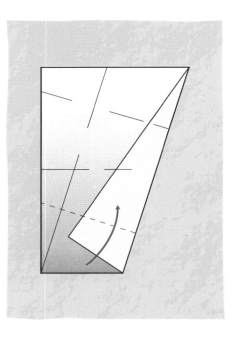

12 ... then refold the existing valley fold-line at the bottom ...

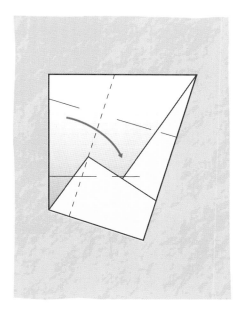

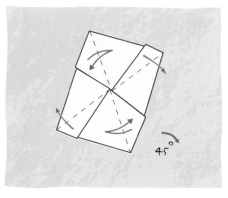

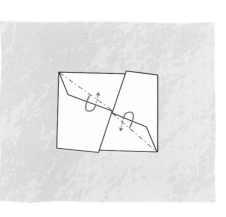

13 ... followed by the existing valley fold-line on the left.

15 Valley fold the top right-hand flap from the centre point out to the corner. Repeat for the bottom left-hand flap. In each case there will be a small triangle of excess paper overhanging the edge. Do the same with the remaining two flaps, this time folding then unfolding. Rotate the model through 45°.

18 Now peak fold and tuck in the flaps along the existing valley fold-lines.

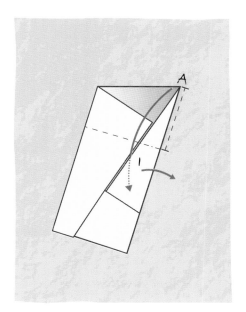

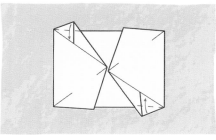

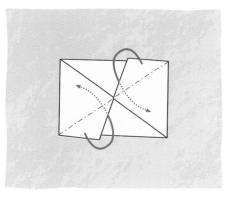

16 Valley fold in the excess flaps of paper at the top and bottom as shown.

19 Finally, peak fold the remaining two flaps along the existing valley fold-lines.

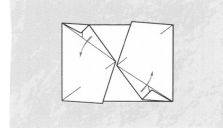

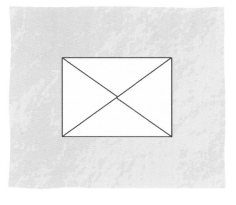

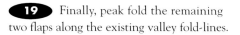

14 Lift up the edge of flap 1 to allow point A to be tucked in underneath it: hold flap 1 open and valley fold the top section down over the existing fold-line and tuck the point underneath the flap. Gently push the point home, then refold flap 1 over it.

17 Now unfold the two flaps in the direction of the arrows, tucking the 'excess' triangles underneath.

20 The completed Foldelope *Shi*. Write the address on the other side.

This is a simple and effective way to display a standard-sized 15 x 10cm (6 x 4in) postcard or photo.

A 'locking' device that you create at the end of the

folding process makes the frame stable.

HORIZONTAL
PICTURE FRAME

The image is displayed

horizontally. You need a sheet of paper measuring 20.5 x 39cm (8 x 15 ¼in). Although the paper should be

firm enough to stay rigid when folded it should not be too thick, otherwise the folds will not be sharp enough. Try

to find paper that enhances the character of the image you intend to frame. Here we have used a beige speckled paper

to complement the colours and textures of the collages.

INSTRUCTIONS FOR HORIZONTAL PICTURE FRAME

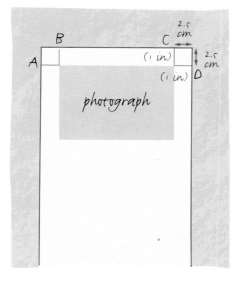

1 Place your picture on the sheet as shown, leaving a margin of paper 2.5cm (1in) wide at the top and sides. With a pencil, lightly mark the four points (marked A B C D on the diagram) on the edges of the sheet, 2.5cm (1in) in from the top corners. Remove the picture.

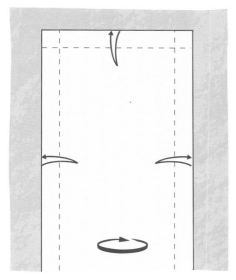

2 Using these marks as guides, valley fold in the top and side edges of the sheet as shown. Press flat and unfold, then turn the sheet over.

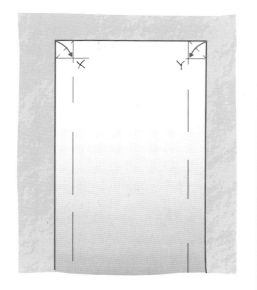

3 Valley fold in the top corners to points X and Y (where the horizontal and vertical valley fold-lines intersect).

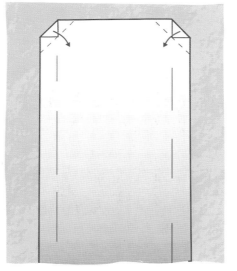

4 Valley fold the two corners in again from the tips of the triangular flaps formed in step 3.

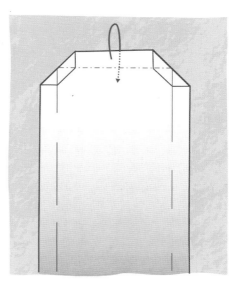

5 Now peak fold along the existing horizontal fold-line.

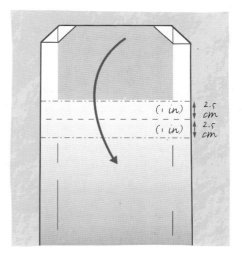

6 Re-insert the picture so that it fits snugly into the top corner flaps. With a pencil, mark the position of the bottom edge of the picture. Make two more marks at intervals of 2.5cm (1in) below the first mark. Remove the picture. Using the pencil marks as guides, fold the sheet as shown above to create three parallel fold-lines: first peak fold the top and bottom lines, press flat and unfold. Then valley fold the middle line and press flat.

INSTRUCTIONS FOR HORIZONTAL PICTURE FRAME

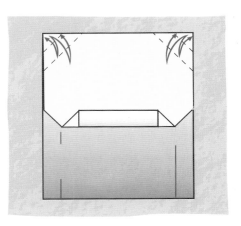

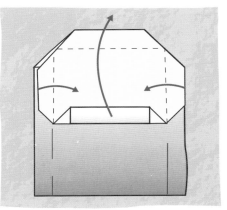

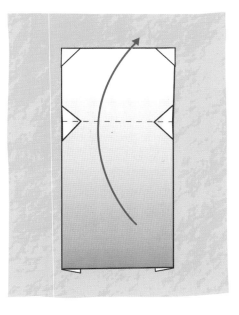

7 Repeat steps 3 and 4 at the top corners. Press flat and unfold.

9 Redefine all the valley fold-lines shown on the top flap. Valley fold in the two vertical sides, then fold back the whole top flap in the direction of the arrow, valley folding along the existing horizontal crease.

11 Valley fold the bottom section up over the top section.

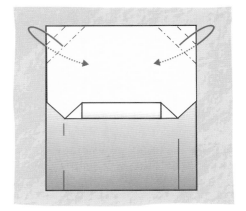

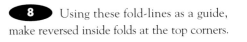

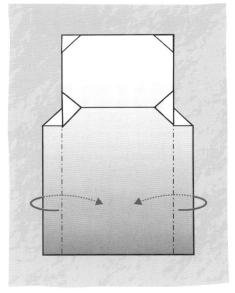

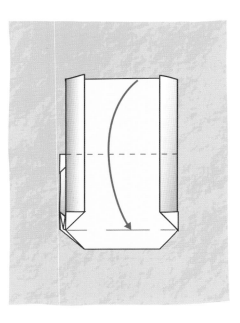

8 Using these fold-lines as a guide, make reversed inside folds at the top corners.

10 Now peak fold the two vertical edges of the bottom section along the existing fold-lines.

12 This is how the model should now look. Valley fold the top edge down to meet the existing horizontal fold-line.

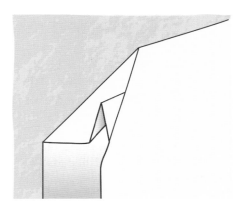

8a The corners should like this.

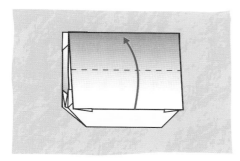

13 Now valley fold the top flap in half, folding upwards.

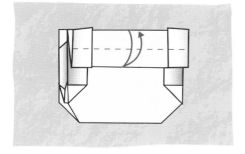

14 Valley fold the flap once more, this time folding downwards. Press flat and open out again.

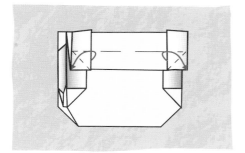

15 Insert your thumbs into the two pockets on either side of the top flap. Draw your thumbs down in a diagonal direction, causing the pockets to open outwards. The lower sections of the pockets will fold back on themselves, creating the diagonal valley folds shown. Press these flat to define them.

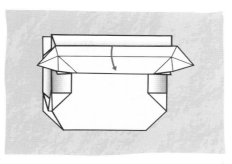

16 As you fold the pockets outwards the top of the flap will start to fold down along the horizontal valley fold-line ...

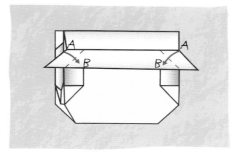

17 ... remove your thumbs and press flat along this fold-line to close the flap, creating the shape shown above. Now valley fold down from point A to point B on the left and right of the model, thus folding in the overhanging triangular corners of the flap.

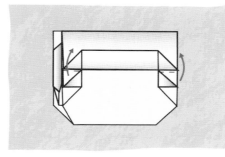

18 Now valley fold the two triangular corners upwards as shown.

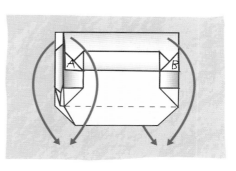

19 Fold the top flap of the model down, folding along the existing fold-line shown. Repeat at the back.

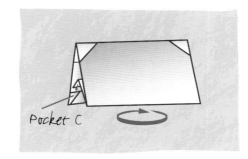

Pocket C

20 Tuck the triangular flaps (marked A and B on diagram 19) into their respective pockets (marked C in this diagram). Then turn the model around.

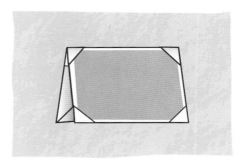

21 The horizontal picture frame is complete. Insert the corners of your picture into the corner flaps.

DOUBLE PICTURE FRAME

This is another simple and attractive way of displaying photographs or other artworks. Here we give instructions for making a frame designed to hold standard-sized postcards or photographs (15 x 10cm or 6 x 4in), but you can adapt the design to fit any size of picture. For this size, start with a sheet of paper measuring about 31.5 x 20cm (12 $\frac{1}{2}$ x 7 $\frac{3}{4}$in). Use stiff paper or thin card to make the frame rigid enough to stand upright, and choose a colour, texture or pattern that will complement your image.

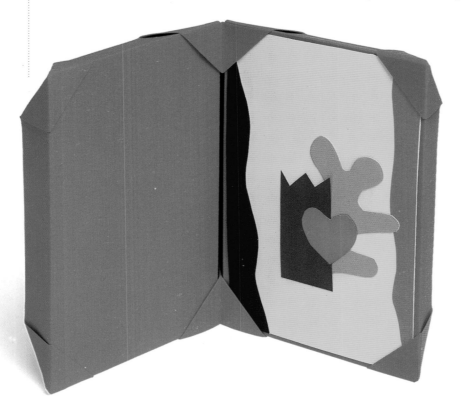

INSTRUCTIONS FOR DOUBLE PICTURE FRAME

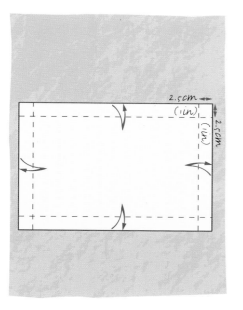

1 Valley fold all four sides of the paper 2.5cm (1in) in from the edges. Press flat and unfold.

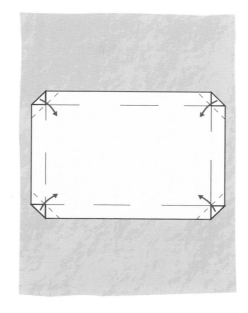

3 Valley fold each corner in again from the points of the triangular flaps to create the shape shown in diagram 4.

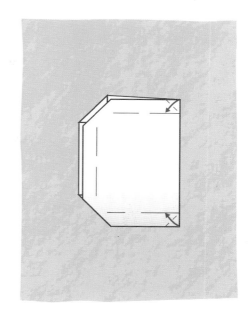

5 Valley fold the top and bottom right-hand corners in to meet the existing horizontal fold-lines.

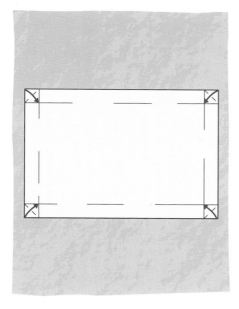

2 Valley fold each corner in to where the horizontal and vertical fold-lines intersect, thus forming small triangular flaps at each corner.

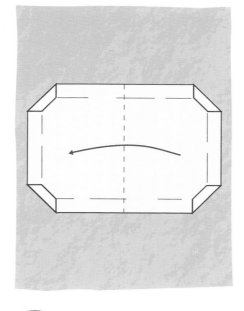

4 Fold the model in half vertically, folding from right to left and making sure all the edges line up accurately.

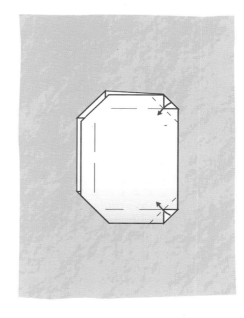

6 Valley fold these corners in again from the points formed by the previous folds. Refer to diagram 7 to see the shape created by this movement.

INSTRUCTIONS FOR DOUBLE PICTURE FRAME

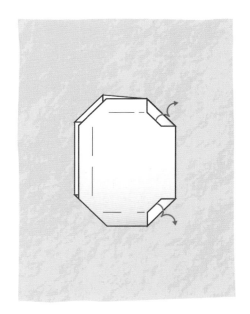

7 Now open out the folds you formed in steps 5 and 6.

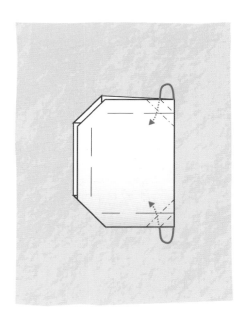
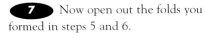

8 Using the fold-lines to guide you, make reversed inside folds (see page 11) at the top and bottom right-hand corners: first make inside folds ...

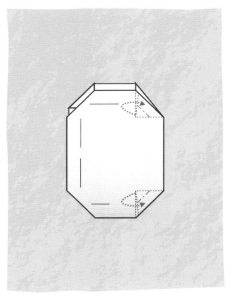

9 ... then open out the corners slightly and push up the small triangular sections as shown to complete the reversed inside folds.

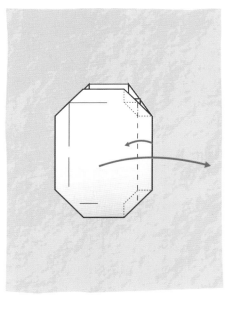

10 Valley fold in the right-hand edge as shown. Then fold back the top flap along this valley fold to form the shape shown in diagram 11.

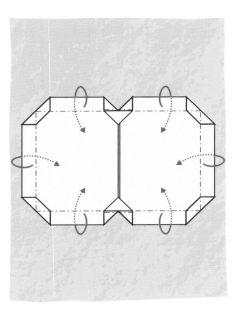

11 Press flat the triangular flaps at the centre of the model. Then peak fold the six flaps indicated by the arrows.

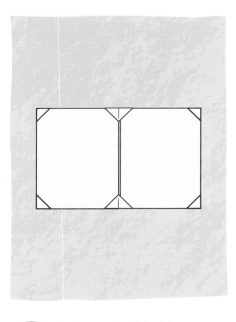

12 The completed double picture frame. Insert the corners of your pictures into the flaps.

FLAPPING BIRD

The flapping bird is an ancient origami design that enchants everyone – especially children – the first time they see it. Not just a clever abstraction of a bird in flight, it is actually a working model: when you pull the bird's breast and tail the wings flap! It is one of the simplest and quickest models to make, and it's a good one to begin with, as the end result is so satisfying. To produce a flapping bird from a sheet of ordinary white paper in a few seconds (once you've practised it) is like doing a baffling conjuring trick.

All you need is a square sheet of paper 16 x 16cm (6 ¹/₄ x 6 ¹/₄in) – this will produce a model about 15 cm (6in) long. Any thin typing or writing paper will do. Start by completing the Crane Base, an easy series of folds which forms the basis of many origami models.

INSTRUCTIONS FOR CRANE BASE

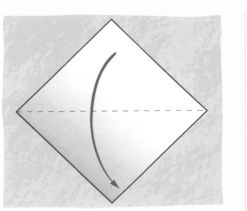

1 Turn the sheet around to form a square diamond shape. Valley fold the paper in half from top to bottom to form an inverted triangle.

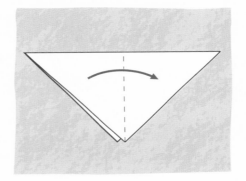

2 Valley fold the triangle in half from left to right.

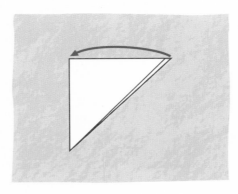

3 Now raise the top (folded) flap to an angle of 90°.

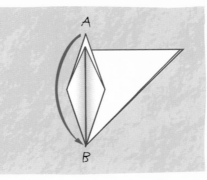

4 Pinch the flap at point A and push it down to meet point B, allowing the sides of the flap to open out fully.

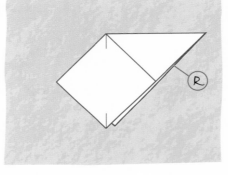

5 Press the paper flat and define the folds to form a square diamond shape as shown here. Turn the model over and repeat steps 3-5.

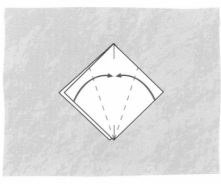

6 (Top layer only) Valley fold the lower left and right edges in to meet the centre fold-line, as shown.

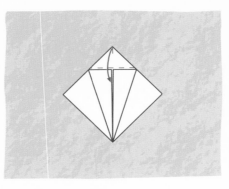

7 Valley fold the upper triangle down over the flaps formed in step 6.

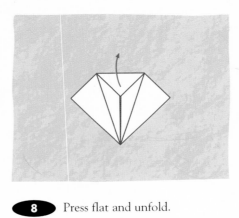

8 Press flat and unfold.

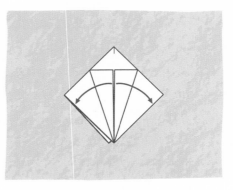

9 Unfold the two flaps previously formed in step 6 to recreate the square diamond shape.

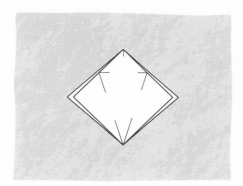

10 Your model should now look like this, with the three fold-lines forming the shape of an inverted isosceles triangle.

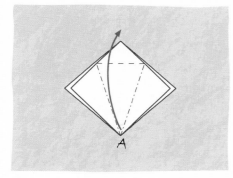

11 Lift the top flap (consisting of a single sheet only) at point A and fold back in the direction of the arrow.

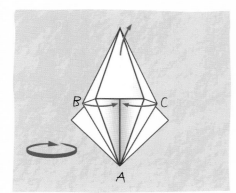

12 Continue folding back the flap until it lies flat; as you do so, points B and C will fold in and come together (press

with your fingertip at point A to keep the remaining layers of paper in place). Press the model flat to form a diamond shape.

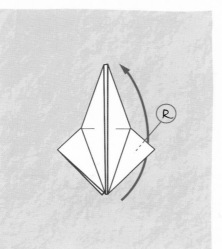

13 Turn the model over and repeat steps 6-12 on the other side.

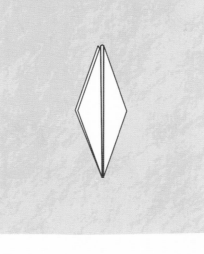

14 The completed crane base.

FLAPPING BIRD

Make sure the Crane Base is the correct way up; the flaps with a concealed triangle in between should be uppermost.

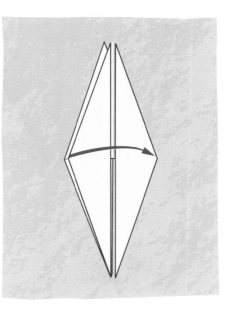

1 Valley fold the left flap (top layer only) over to the right.

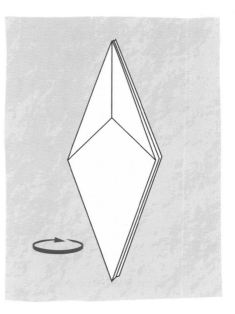

2 This should be the result. Now turn the model over.

FLAPPING BIRD

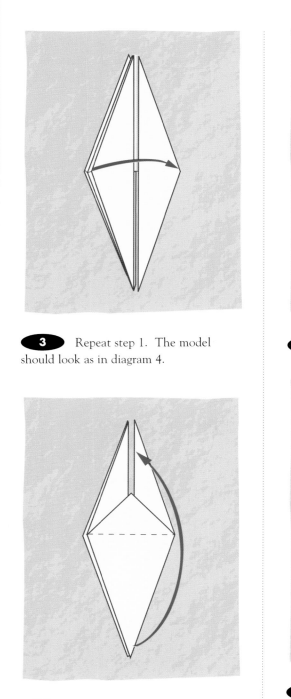

3 Repeat step 1. The model should look as in diagram 4.

4 Valley fold the bottom point (top layer only) up over the top points, folding along the existing crease.

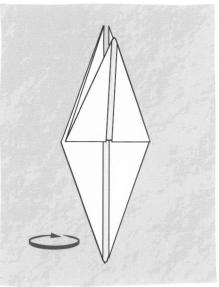

5 Turn the model over.

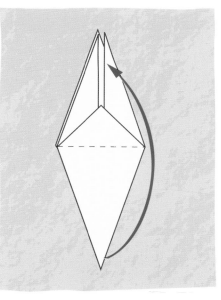

6 Repeat step 4, creating the shape illustrated in diagram 7.

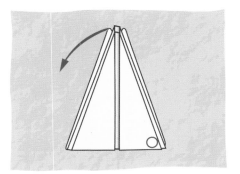

7 Pinch the bottom right corner of the model. Then pinch the tip of the inner flap on the left and pull it down ...

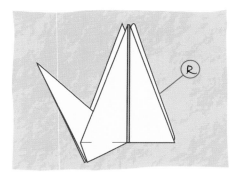

8 ... to the position shown here (stop when the inner fold at the base reverses in on itself). Crease firmly at the bottom. This forms the bird's neck. Repeat steps 7-8 on the right-hand side to form the tail.

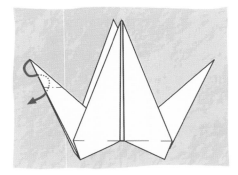

9 Make an inside fold near the top of the bird's neck to form the head.

10 Valley fold the upmost wing down, making a diagonal fold as shown.

12 Unfold the wings again. Your flapping bird is now complete.

13 Hold the model at the base of the neck. Pull and push the tail to make the wings flap.

11 Repeat for the other wing.

One of the many ways in which you can put your origami skills to use is by making your own greetings cards, as shown here. To make this card, simply glue some contrasting coloured paper onto a card. Make the flapping bird up to step 10 and glue it onto the front of the card.

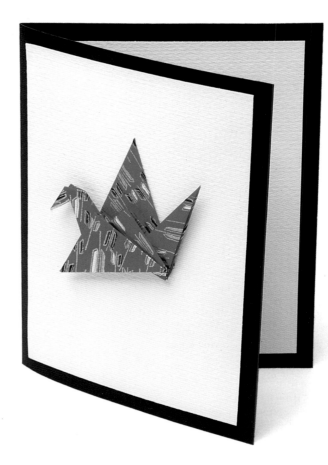

41

FURTHER FOLDS

✸ IN THIS CHAPTER WE SHOW YOU SOME SLIGHTLY MORE ADVANCED PROJECTS.

✸ THEY LEAD ON NATURALLY FROM THE MODELS IN THE PREVIOUS CHAPTER, SO YOU WILL FIND THAT YOU HAVE ALREADY LEARNT THE SKILLS YOU NEED. ✸ THE SIMPLEST PROJECT IN THIS CHAPER IS THE JUMPING FROGS – VERY POPULAR WITH CHILDREN!

✸ YOU WILL ALSO SEE HOW VERSATILE ORIGAMI CAN BE – WE SHOW YOU A RANGE OF CONTAINERS, FROM A COMPUTER DISK HOLDER TO A VARIED SELECTION OF ATTRACTIVE AND UNUSUAL BOXES. ✸

JUMPING FROG

Another simple design, these frogs are quick to make. The folds along their backs act like a spring – make the frogs jump by pressing and releasing them like tiddlywinks. With a set of frogs in different colours, several players can play 'froggiwinks', making the frogs jump into the bowl.

(This is an origami design, too; see instructions on page 47). As the players become more skilled you can increase the distance from starting line to bowl - the frogs are surprisingly springy!

It's best to use quite thick paper – I suggest 175gsm – to make your models more resilient. Start with a sheet around 12.5cm (5in) square to make models 7.5cm (3in) long.

INSTRUCTIONS FOR JUMPING FROG

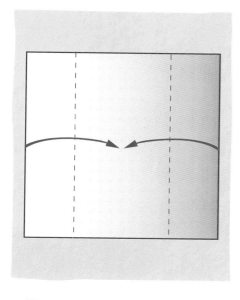

1 Valley fold the left and right edges in to meet in the middle.

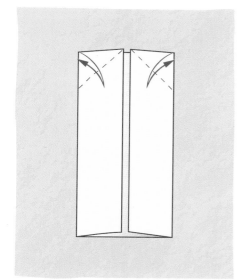

2 Valley fold the top left and right corners in to meet at the centre line. Press down and open out again, forming diagonal creases as shown.

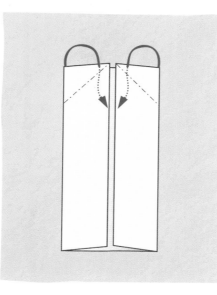

3 Using these valley folds as guides, make inside folds (see page 10) at the top left and right corners.

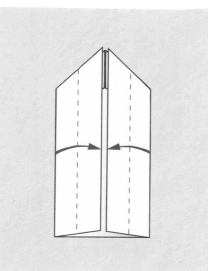

4 Valley fold the left and right edges in to meet at the centre line.

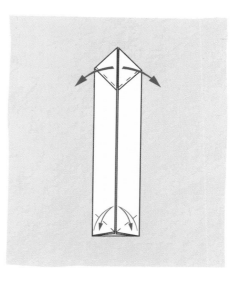

5 Pull the two pointed flaps at the top of the model down in the direction of the arrows and valley fold to form 'wings' (see diagram 6).

At the base of the model, valley fold the bottom left and right edges up to meet the centre line. Smooth down the folds and open out again.

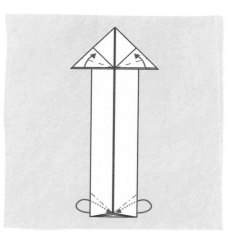

6 Valley fold the two 'wings' at the top of the model in half as shown, to create the shapes shown in diagram 7. These are the frog's front legs.

At the base of the model make inside folds at left and right, using the existing valley fold-lines to guide you.

INSTRUCTIONS FOR JUMPING FROG

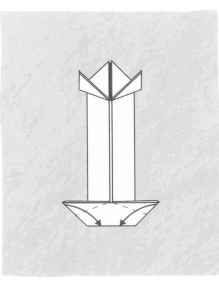

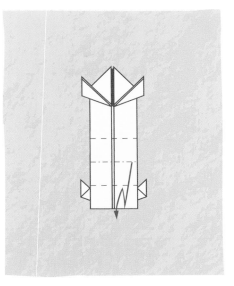

7 Now grasp the two flaps at the base and pull them up and out until they lie flat. As you do so, the bottom section will fold upwards, creating the shape shown in diagram 8. Press flat.

8 Valley fold the base flaps as shown to create the frog's back legs.

10 Now pleat fold the frog's body as shown in the diagram, making first a valley, then a peak, then a valley fold. Make sure the pleats are sharp and that they line up neatly one over the other. This pleating forms the 'spring' mechanism that makes the frog jump.

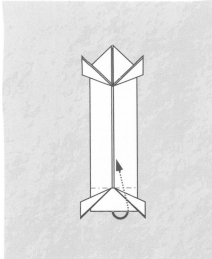

9 Make a horizontal peak fold at the point where the back legs meet.

11 The completed jumping frog. Press firmly at the base of the model and release to make the frog jump.

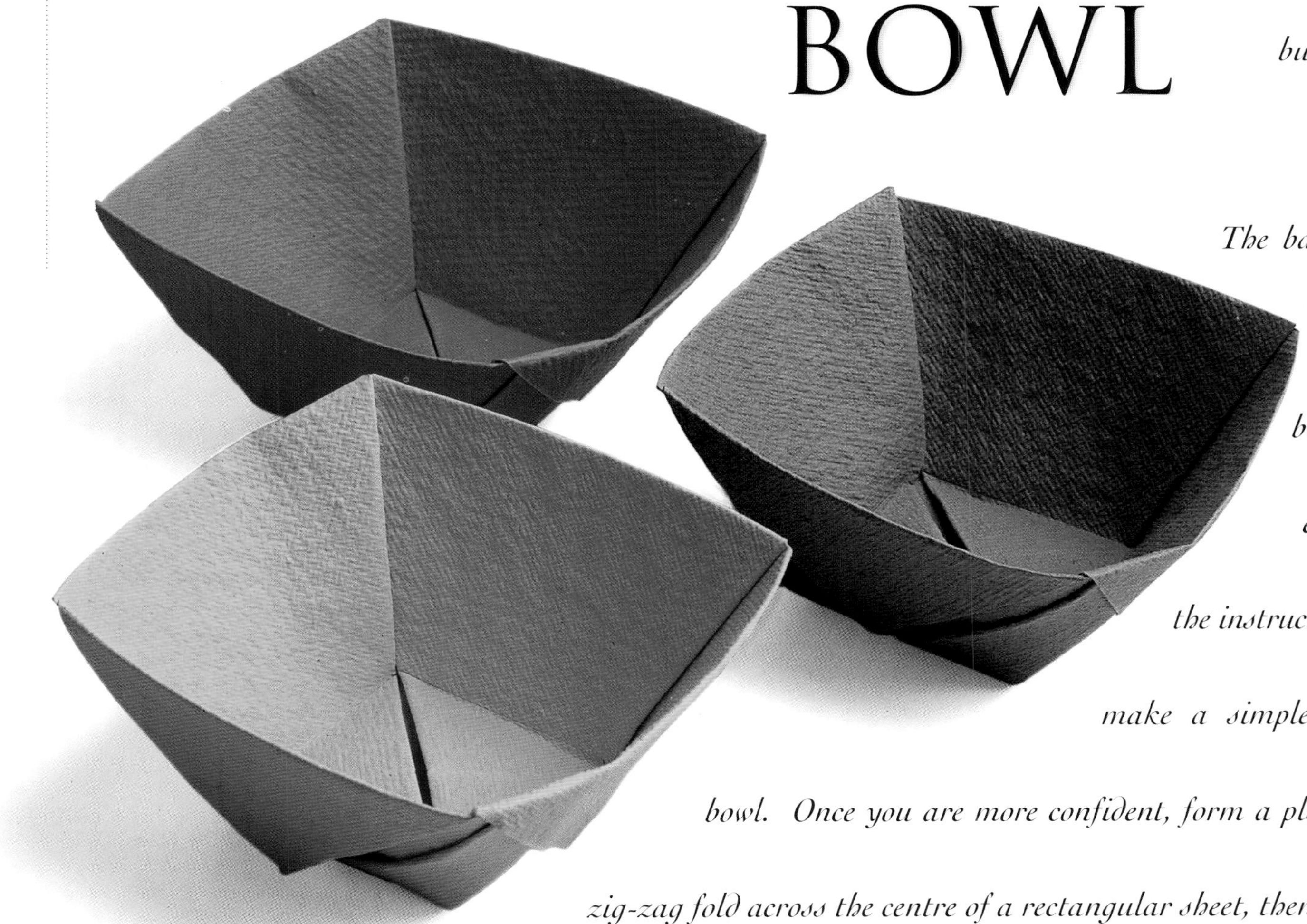

The sculptural shape and inherent strength derived from the construction makes this bowl both elegant and functional. It's even robust enough to use as an eating vessel – though you should choose undyed paper that won't seep colour on to the food, and remember that it isn't water-tight. More likely, you'll use it as

FOUR-SIDED BOWL

a decorative container. We have shown it on page 44, used for froggiwinks, but you can put it to many uses. The bases of the bowls shown here have been pleated for extra durability; the instructions overleaf will make a simpler, flat-bottomed bowl. Once you are more confident, form a pleat by making a zig-zag fold across the centre of a rectangular sheet, then begin folding as normal. It's best to use thick paper or card; to make a bowl of about 13cm (5in) in diameter, you will need an A4 sheet of paper measuring 210 x 297mm (8 $^1/_4$ x 11 $^3/_4$ in.).

INSTRUCTIONS FOR FOUR-SIDED BOWL

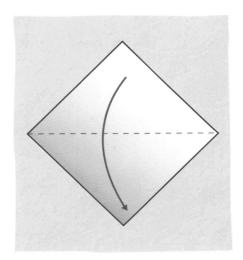

1 Turn the sheet around to form a square diamond shape. Valley fold from top to bottom.

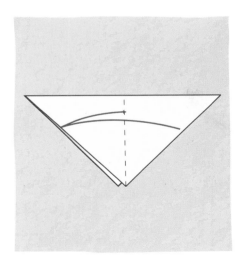

2 Valley fold from right to left, then unfold the top sheet back so it stands at a 90° angle (see diagram 3).

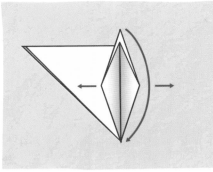

3 Open the mouth of the flap and squash the top point down to meet the bottom point. Press flat, creating a square diamond shape (see diagram 4).

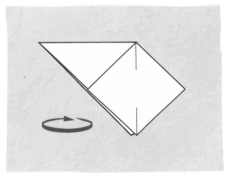

4 Turn the model over.

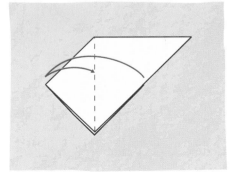

5 Valley fold the top sheet from right to left along the existing vertical fold-line. Unfold the flap back until it is at a 90° angle.

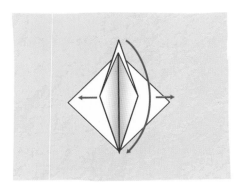

6 Repeat step 3 to create a square diamond shape.

7 Valley fold the top sheet in half from bottom to top. Press flat and open out again.

8 Valley fold the top point of the model to meet the centre fold-line. Press flat and unfold.

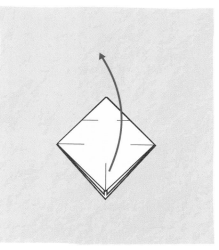

9 Lift the top sheet in the direction of the arrow and open the model out completely, once again forming a square diamond shape.

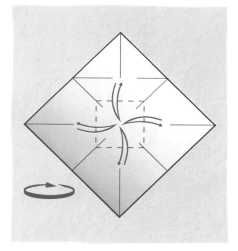

10 Redefine the four fold-lines that form a square in the centre of the sheet by valley folding them in, pressing them flat and unfolding them. Turn the sheet over.

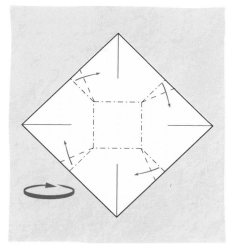

11 Redefine as peak folds the four fold-lines that radiate outwards from the corners of the inner square. Now press with your finger at one of the corners, lift the paper up at the edge and draw the peak fold over in the direction of the arrow until it lies flat. Press the paper flat to form a valley fold. Repeat on the remaining corners. Turn the model over.

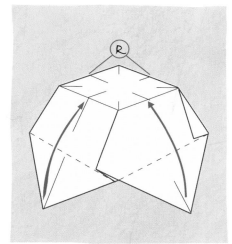

12 Check that the corner folds made in step 11 are parallel with the fold-lines running down the centre of each side of the bowl and adjust them if necessary. Valley fold each of the pointed flaps in so that its point meets the base of the bowl.

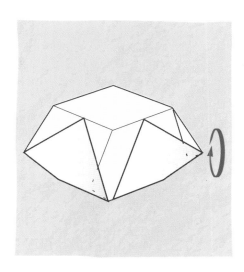

13 This is how your model should now look, with the flaps made in step 12 overlapping the corner folds made in step 11. Turn the model over.

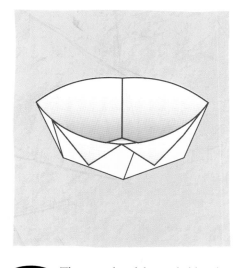

14 The completed four-sided bowl.

LOTUS
BOWL

This beautiful bowl is called 'The Lotus' becuase its harmonious symmetry and petal-like edges

echo the shape of the lotus flower, sacred to many cultures.

A development from the four-sided bowl shown previously, it is a stronger construction and is even

capable of holding water. (During World War II, American airmen were taught an origami design for a cup in

case they were brought down behind enemy lines without a vessel to contain water — an ironic tribute to the

resourcefulness of their Japanese enemy...)

INSTRUCTIONS FOR LOTUS BOWL

Begin by completing steps 1-12 of the Four-Sided Bowl (see page 48).

1 Having defined the valley folds shown here on each side of the bowl, unfold the four flaps again. Valley fold the point of each flap to meet the fold-line already defined.

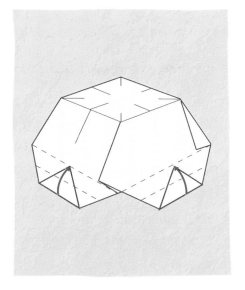

2 Valley fold the edge of each flap to the first fold-line.

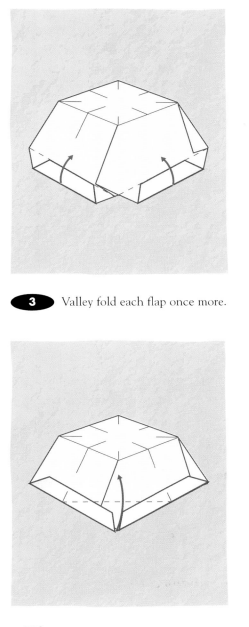

3 Valley fold each flap once more.

4 Now valley fold horizontally across each corner of the bowl as shown. Each of these folds should begin at the base of one of the existing vertical fold-lines and end at the base of the one next to it (see above).

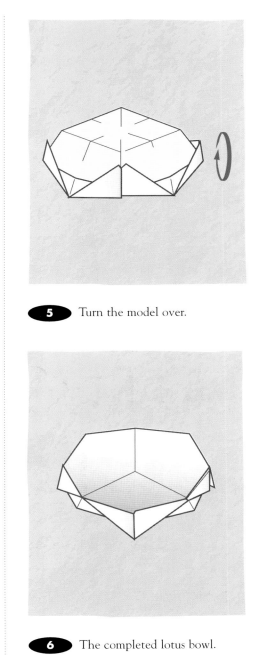

5 Turn the model over.

6 The completed lotus bowl.

This gift bag is one of the most versatile and popular projects in the book. Easy to make and surpringly strong, it makes a perfect container for all kinds of small gifts.

GIFT BAG

As long as your paper is not too thick (a maximum weight of 175gsm is recommended) you can really let your imagination run as wild as your budget will allow when choosing a suitable paper. We used hand-made marbled sheets, available from specialist art shops, but remember that much of the fun of origami is in finding or making your own favourite patterned papers to suit your purpose.

To make a small bag about 6cm (2 ¹/2 in) high, start with a sheet of paper about 18.5cm (7 ¹/4 in) square.

INSTRUCTIONS FOR GIFT BAG

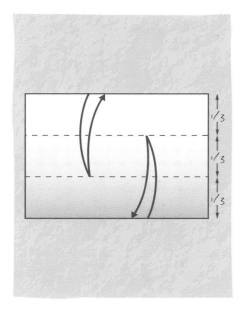

1 Place the sheet sideways and valley fold it horizontally into thirds. Unfold the sheet.

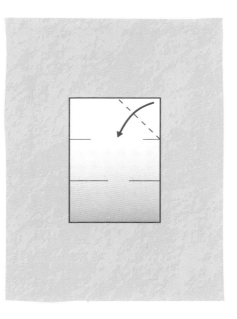

3 Valley fold the top right-hand corner down to meet the first horizontal fold-line, forming a triangular flap.

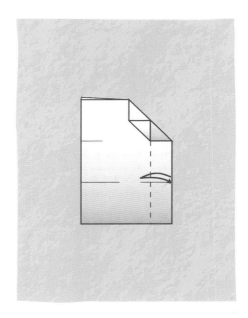

5 Now make a vertical valley fold, in line with the vertical edge of the triangular flap. Press flat and unfold.

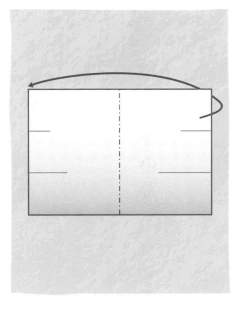

2 Peak fold the sheet vertically in half from right to left, as shown.

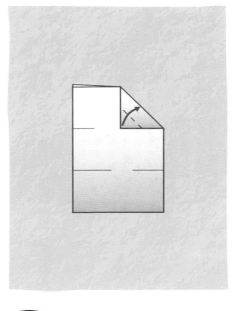

4 Valley fold the tip of the triangular flap up to meet the outside edge.

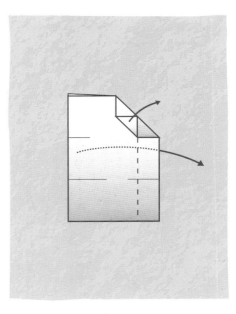

6 Open out the folds in the top right corner, then unfold the back sheet in the direction of the arrow so that the paper lies flat.

INSTRUCTIONS FOR GIFT BAG

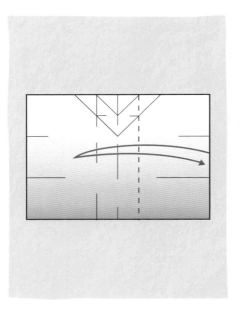

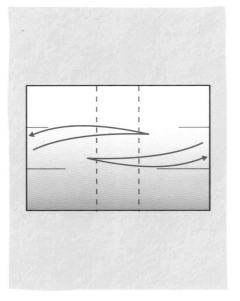

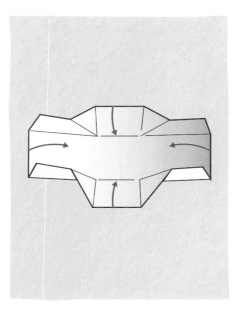

7 Your unfolded sheet should now look like this. The diagonal folds that you created at the top of the sheet were made in order to gauge the two vertical lines which will form the base of your bag. The diagonal fold-lines will not be shown on the diagrams that follow.

9 Define both vertical folds as valley folds. Open out the sheet.

11 Now bring all four sides in to a vertical, one at a time...

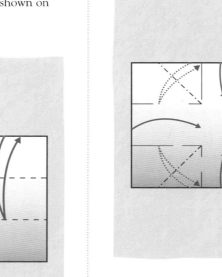

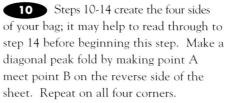

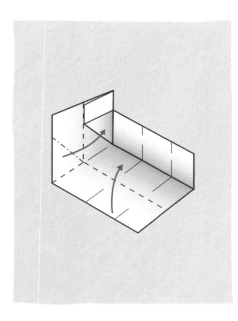

8 Define the two previously made horizontal folds as valley folds.

10 Steps 10-14 create the four sides of your bag; it may help to read through to step 14 before beginning this step. Make a diagonal peak fold by making point A meet point B on the reverse side of the sheet. Repeat on all four corners.

12 ...you will find as you bring up the first side that a corner forms naturally, as you have already defined the necessary peak fold in step 10. Now repeat this movementon the other side to make the shape shown in the next diagram.

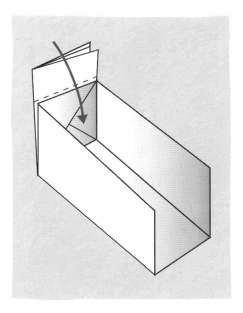

13 Secure this side by valley folding the top flap down as shown.

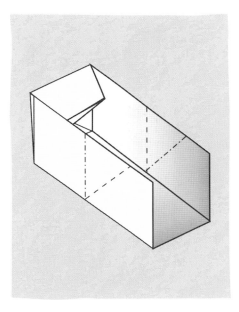

14 Now repeat steps 12 and 13 on the other side of the bag.

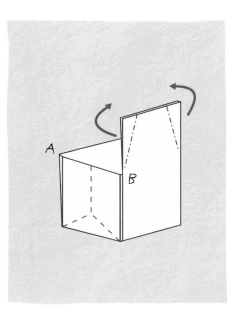

15 Pinch together the top of the sides of the bag and define the valley folds in the bag that this movement creates. Next taper the edges of the top flap by folding in two peak folds. This forms the 'lid' of the bag.

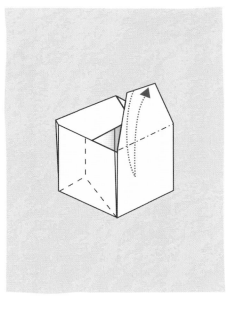

16 Now create a horizontal peak fold in line with the top of the bag and unfold again.

17 Now insert the flap into the flap opposite as shown...

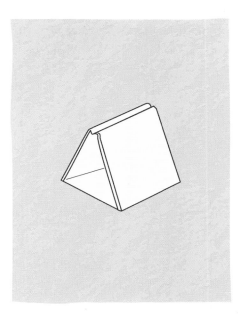

18 ...and the gift bag is completed.

DISK HOLDER

The ancient art of origami can have totally up-to-date applications,

as this simple and stylish disk holder shows. A set of holders in different colours on your desk will look much more

decorative than a plastic box! The design resembles that of the Gift Bag but has concertina-like pleats which form

slots that keep the disks cushioned and separated. You will need a sheet of card or stiff paper approximately

A3 size (29.7 x 42cm or 11 ³/4 x 16 ¹/2 in) to make a container for six standard floppy disks.

INSTRUCTIONS FOR DISK HOLDER

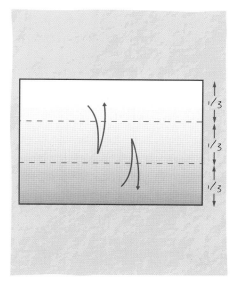

1 Place the sheet of paper sideways on. Valley fold it horizontally into thirds and unfold the sheet.

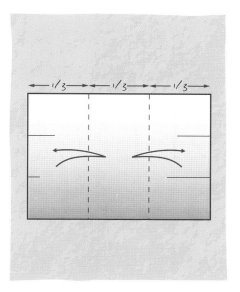

2 Valley fold the sheet vertically into thirds and unfold so that it lies flat.

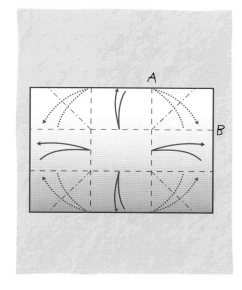

3 Now create the folds that will make the corners of the box using the same technique you learned in step 10 of the gift bag (see page 54). Make point A meet point B on the reverse of the sheet and fold in the resulting peak fold. Repeat this process for all the corners, as shown. Unfold the sheet flat again.

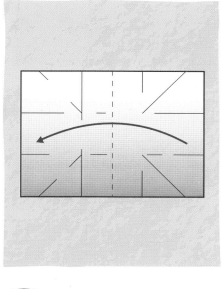

4 Fold the sheet in half vertically from right to left.

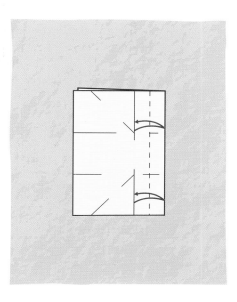

5 Make a valley fold from the right edge to the existing fold-line. Press flat and unfold.

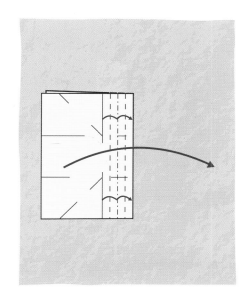

6 Make two more vertical valley folds half way between the existing fold-lines. Unfold them. You should now have five vertical fold-lines. Open the model out again.

INSTRUCTIONS FOR DISK HOLDER

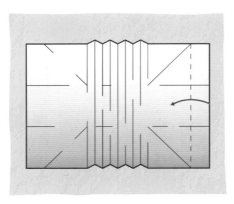

7   To form the concertina, redefine the folds you have made so they alternate between valley and peak folds. Make sure the first and last folds are valley folds. Valley fold the right-hand edge vertically in the direction of the arrow.

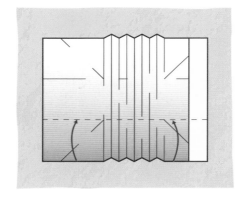

8   Valley fold the bottom edge up to a perpendicular position.

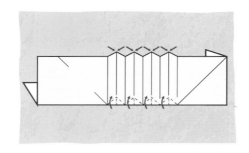

9   Now create the concertina effect by pinching the peak folds together one at

a time at the top, then pressing up and in the valley folds created by this process at the bottom of the model. Now pinch the peak folds together at the bottom. This will give neat edges to the sides of your box. Repeat steps 8-9 on the other side.

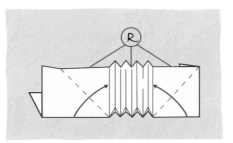

10   Now create the sides of the box by valley folding in the four diagonal lines you created at step 3.

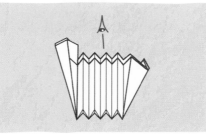

11   Move the four sides of the box to a perpendicular position.

12   One side of the box has a folded-in edge. Tuck the left folded-in edge under the right flap. This will make the side of the

box secure. At the other end fold the right side in then the left side over it. This will form the lid.

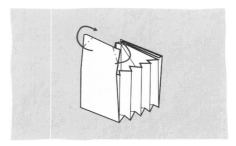

13   Peak fold the corners of the lid as shown, to form a tongue shape.

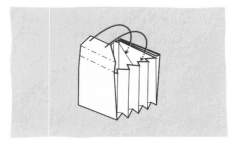

14   Gently define the two peak folds in the top flap as shown. Insert the flap into the slot to close the box.

15   Your completed computer disk portfolio. Insert a disk into each pocket.

STRIP BOX

This extraordinarily clever way of constructing a box out of a strip of paper was suggested by a friend who had seen someone making a container by folding reeds in a similar way. To make a box with a diameter of about 10cm (4in) you will need a strip of paper measuring 66cm (26in) long and 5cm (2in) wide. I used thick but soft-textured paper – stiff paper or card would not be easy to handle for this technique, which involves wrapping and folding at the same time.

Once you have found out how to make this model you can experiment with longer strips to make even more ingenious and elaborate geometric shapes. If you make the first folds crisp and accurate you'll find the box virtually falls into shape as you fold it.

INSTRUCTIONS FOR STRIP BOX

1 Place the sheet horizontally. Valley fold the top left-hand corner in the direction of the arrow as shown, at an angle of about 30°.

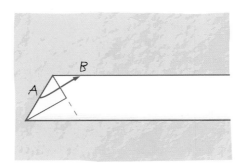

2 Now make another valley fold by bringing up line A as shown so that it is aligned with line B.

3 You have created an upside down equilateral triangle. Peak fold along the line shown, so that the triangle ends up behind the sheet.

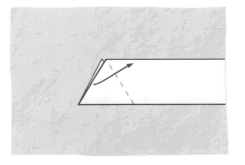

4 Now make a valley fold as shown, using the same technique as in step 2. Use the edge of the triangular shape underneath the sheet as the line to fold along.

5 Peak fold along the line shown, folding the triangle underneath the sheet as in step 3. Now repeat steps 3-5 along the remainder of the strip.

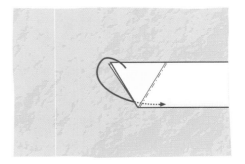

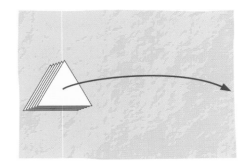

6 You now have a 'concertina' of triangular shapes. Next unfold the model completely, so it looks as it did in step 1.

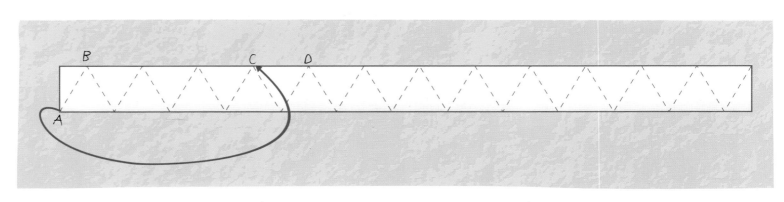

7 You should now have 24 triangles with two half-triangles at either end. If not, cut the strip so that you do. Define all the folds as valley folds. Now curl the strip round so that point A rests on point C. Point B should rest on point D. The small triangle originally at the end of the strip should protrude at the top of the model, as shown in the next diagram.

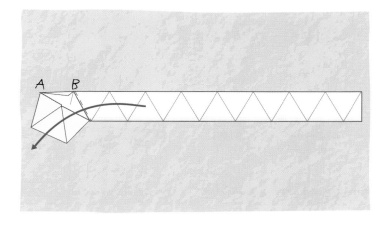

8 Make sure you keep a firm hold on points A and B, and valley fold the strip over in the direction of the arrow. The strip will go naturally in this direction. You should now begin to see the pentagonal shape of the box.

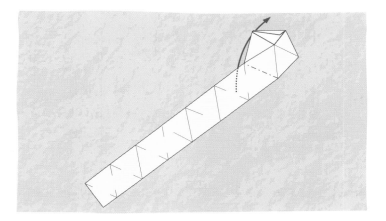

9 Wrap the strip underneath the model in the direction of the arrow shown, covering the top left-hand segment of the shape. The strip will still be wrapping round the model naturally if you are holding the original points A and B firmly in place.

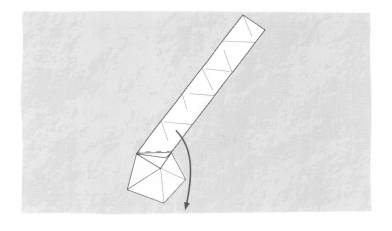

10 Valley fold the next part of the strip over the model.

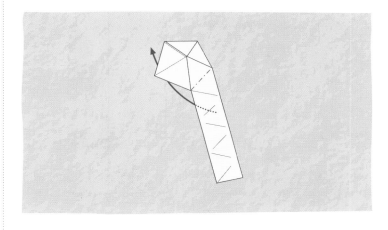

11 Continue by wrapping the strip underneath the model.

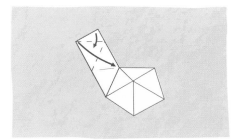

12 Valley fold in the small triangle at the end of the strip. Then make another valley fold in the strip as shown.

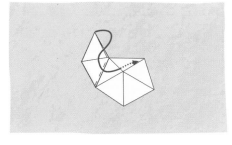

13 Take the point shown at the base of the arrow and insert it into the pocket shown at the arrow's point.

14 Your finished strip box.

The All-in-one box is so called because the hinge, lid and base are all made out of a single piece of paper. A satisfyingly neat object, it makes a perfect presentation box for gifts large and small.

ALL-IN-ONE BOX

It can contain small pieces of jewellery such as cuff-links or earrings, while a larger version is just right for holding a pen or a watch.

The boxes in the picture are made from an unusual art deco-inspired paper, but you should be guided by the design and colour of your gift when choosing paper for the box. If you don't find something that seems quite right you can always create your own pattern or design on plain-coloured paper with marbling, stencilling, stamping or any other decorative paint technique.

An A4 sheet of paper measuring 210 x 297 mm (8 1/4 x 11 3/4 in.) will make a box about 10cm (4in) long.

INSTRUCTIONS FOR ALL-IN-ONE BOX

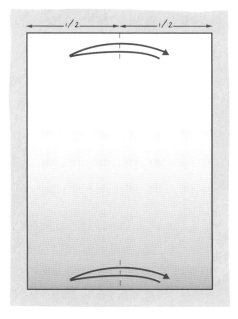

1 Mark the centre of the sheet of paper by taking the right edge to meet the left. Pinch the top and bottom of the sheet; do not define the fold all the way down.

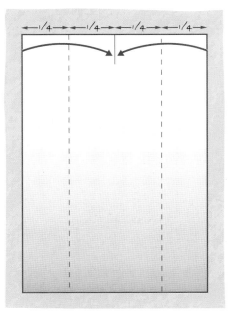

2 Valley fold in both sides of the sheet to meet at the centre line marked in the previous step.

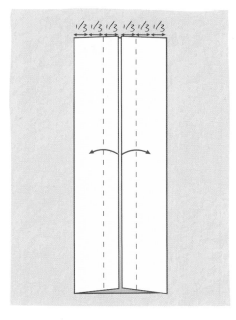

3 Divide both top flaps into thirds and mark each flap top and bottom. Make two vertical valley folds as shown, starting from the centre of the model and following the direction of the arrows.

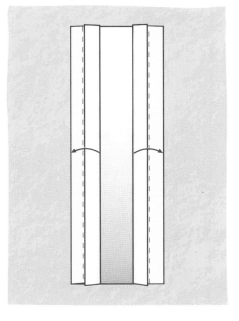

4 Make two more vertical valley folds as shown above.

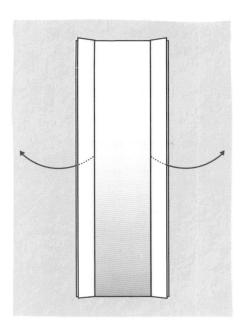

5 Now open out the sheet so that the paper lies flat.

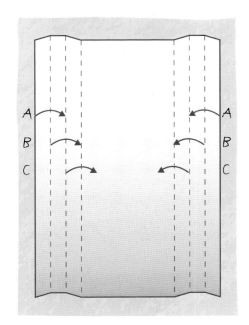

6 Refold all the vertical folds in the order shown. First take point A to the the fold-line shown, then continue with folds B and C.

INSTRUCTIONS FOR ALL-IN-ONE BOX

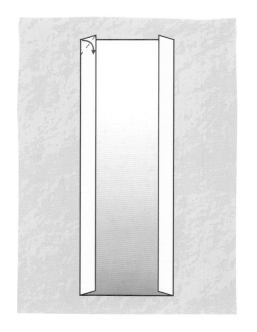

7 Valley fold in the top left-hand corner in the direction of the arrow to make a small flap.

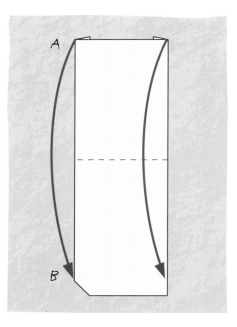

9 Valley fold the model in half, taking point A to point B.

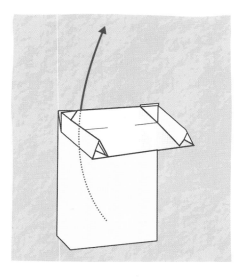

11 With the model in this position, lift up the bottom flap in the direction of the arrow as shown.

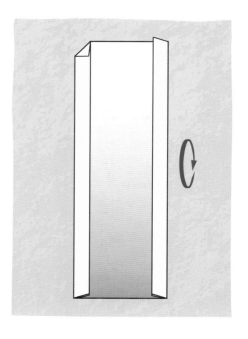

8 Turn the model over in the direction of the arrow.

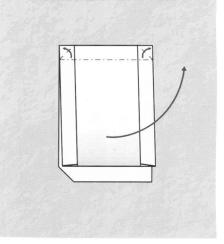

10 Starting at the left-hand corner, make a small diagonal valley fold in the direction of the arrow. As you make this fold, the top flap will rise and take the shape of the base of a box, as shown in the next diagram. Repeat this valley fold in the right-hand corner.

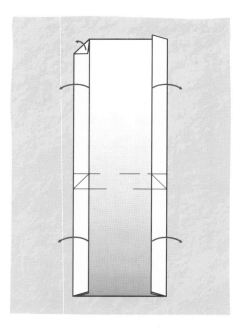

12 Flatten the model. Now open out the the top left corner and unfold once each side of the model so that it looks as in step 13.

These earrings are prettily packed in the All-in-One Box on a bed of shredded tissue paper which you can buy ready prepared or make yourself very easily. Alternatives might be coloured cotton wool or a scrap of silk or velvet.

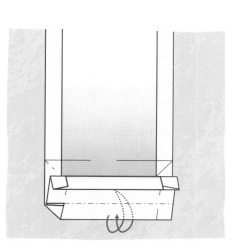

16 Now fold back the peak fold as shown, using the top edge of the flap made in the last step as a marker.

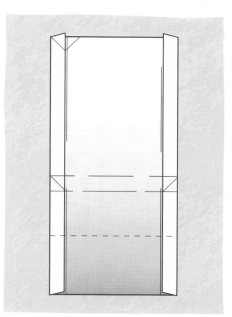

13 Valley fold up the bottom edge so that it aligns with the higher of the two existing fold-lines.

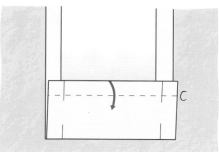

14 Using the lower fold-line (marked C) as a guide, valley fold the model down in the direction of the arrow.

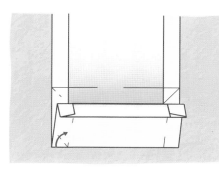

15 Valley fold in the bottom left-hand corner as shown, making a small flap.

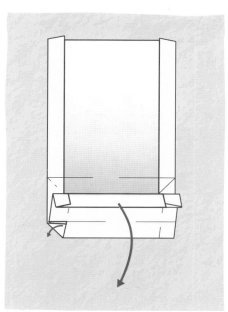

17 First unfold the flap at the bottom left-hand corner, following the small arrow. Then unfold the model in the direction of the arrow.

INSTRUCTIONS FOR ALL-IN-ONE BOX

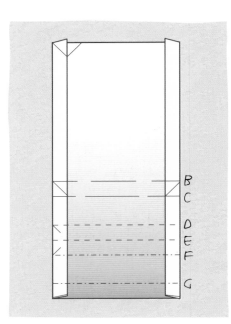

18 Define valley fold-lines at points D and E, then define peak fold-lines at lines G and F.

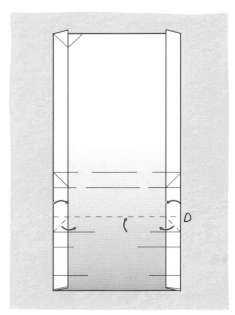

19 Lift up the two sides of the model so they are at 90° to the 'floor' of the model. Now make a valley fold at line D. As you do this, bring the bottom two

side flaps inwards and flatten them. Bring the top flap up to 90°, defining the two small diagonal peak folds at the corners as shown. These two movements create hinges at the corners of the box.

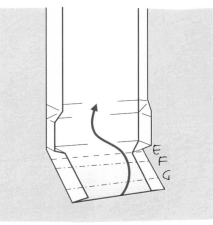

20 The paper from the bottom edge to line E creates a lining for the box. Make a valley fold at line E. Bring the bottom flap up then define the two peak folds at lines F and G. Tuck the paper into the base of the box to form the lining.

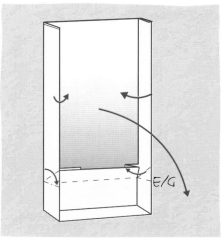

21 Line G now lies on top of line E. Valley fold down the top of the model at this line until the top is at right angles

to the bottom. Bring in the two side flaps at the top of the model and flatten them. This will create a peak and valley fold at each corner. Define these to make hinges.

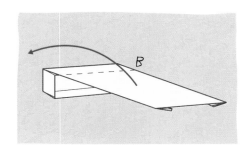

22 The model should now look like this. Valley fold the top of the model along line B in the direction of the arrow.

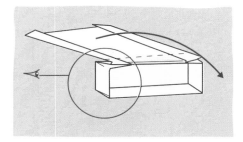

23 Now begin to valley fold the top sheet back in the direction of the arrow. The fold line should be nearly, but not quite, in line with the base of the box.

24 This is a side view of the model as you complete step 23. It is important that the fold you have just made does not quite reach back to the base of the box as shown here, and that you do not fully define this fold, leaving it slightly rounded.

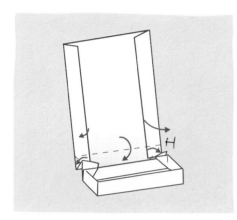

25 Make a valley fold at line H by bringing the top of the model down in the direction of the central arrow. Unfold it out. Now fold out the side flaps of the top part of the model and refold the valley fold you have just made. This time, you will have created a flap at each corner. Make hinges as before by making small valley folds at each corner in the direction of the arrows. Refer to the next diagram to see how the model should look.

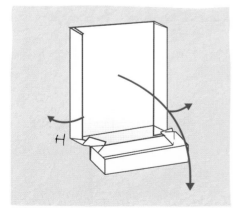

26 Now bring the lid forward over the base of the box, bringing out the sides of the lid as you do so.

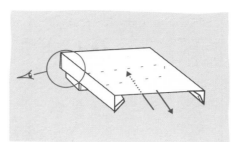

27 Push the base of the box back and pull the lid forward so it fits snugly. Now examine the box from the side as indicated above.

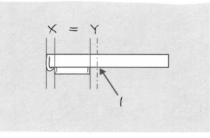

28 This is a side view of the model. Measure the distance between the edge of the lid and the base of the box (shown as X above). Now define a peak fold so that the two distances X and Y are equal. This is shown as line I.

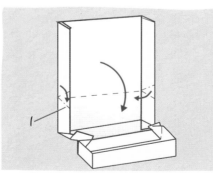

29 Valley fold the top of the model down at line I as shown. Now make a small valley fold at one corner. The peak fold you defined in the last step will fall into place. Repeat at the other corner.

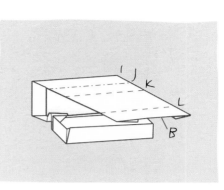

30 Complete the peak fold at line J first, then make valley folds at lines K and L, to form the lining of the lid. As in step 20, tuck the flap snugly into the lid.

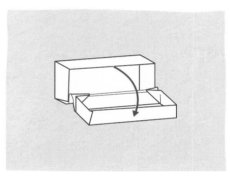

31 Bring the lid over the base in the direction of the arrow to shut the box.

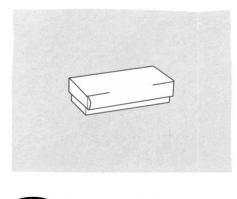

32 The completed All-in-one box.

This is a neat and attractive rectangular box with CARD BOX

an ingenious integral hinged lid that locks tightly when you close the box.

To make the box shown here, which contains a standard set of playing cards, start with an A4 sheet

of paper measuring 210 x 297 mm (8 $^{1}/_{4}$ x 11 $^{3}/_{4}$ in.). You need to use fairly stiff paper or thin card to maintain

the rigidity of the construction. Here we have made the box in a distinctive textured paper with metallic flecks

which complements beautifully the colours of the unusual and decorative Japanese cards.

INSTRUCTIONS FOR CARD BOX

1 Find the centre of the sheet: roll the top left corner over to the top right corner and line up the edges. Run your finger along the top of the sheet and pinch the rounded edge to mark the centre. Open out the sheet.

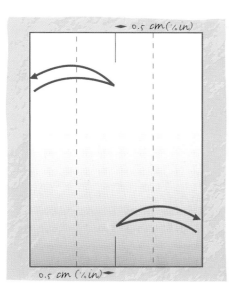

2 Valley fold in the left edge to lie 0.5cm (¼in) past the centre mark made in step 1. Repeat on the right edge. Open out the sheet.

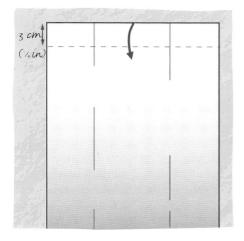

3 Make a valley fold 3cm (1¼in) in from the top edge of the sheet.

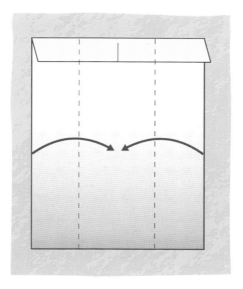

4 Refold the valley folds you created at step 2.

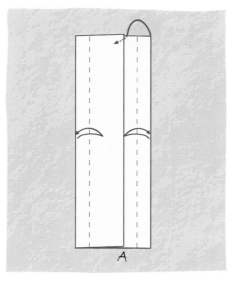

5 Valley fold the right edge over to meet the raw edge (A), forming a panel. Measure the width of the panel, then valley fold the left edge in to form another panel, making sure it is the same width as the first one. There should be a narrow gap between the panels. Now open them out again.

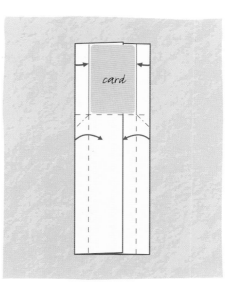

6 Place a pack of playing cards on the centre section of the model, just below the top edge. Keep the cards in place and valley fold in the two side panels while at the same time valley folding the bottom flap up to a 90° angle. Flatten it against the base of the pack, tucking in the side panels so that they too fold up against the base. Press flat to create the two diagonal peak folds shown in the diagram.

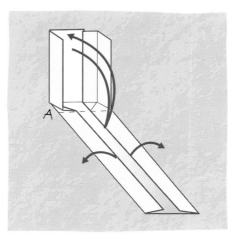

7 Remove the cards. Valley fold along line A (ie. from the base of the peak folds formed in step 6). Open out the side panels and define the valley fold further.

INSTRUCTIONS FOR CARD BOX

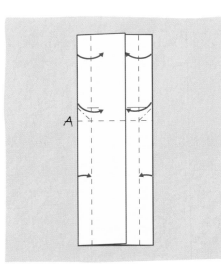

8 Now form the hinges at the back of the box. Fold in the two vertical valley folds you have already made. Then make the valley fold shown at A. As you do this, make sure that the sides of the bottom two-thirds of the model are perpendicular. This will cause two diagonal peak folds to form at the junction between the base and the lid. Define the folds so that the model looks as in diagram 9.

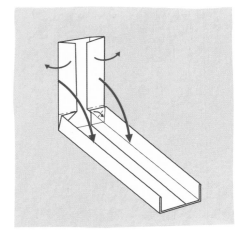

9 Make a diagonal valley fold at each side of the box as shown. This movement naturally brings down the lid and pushes out the sides of the box Press the corner firmly into place.

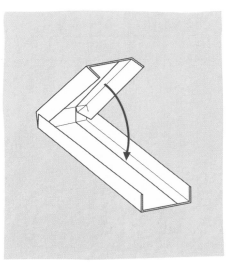

10 Push the lid down inside the base.

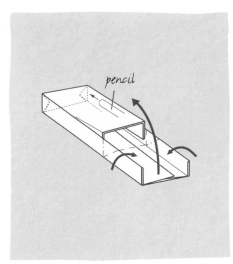

11 Slide a pencil along the inside edges of the box and press to ensure that the hinges are lying flat. Mark the position of the open end of the box with a valley fold (open out the side panels and fold across the whole sheet). Press flat and open out, then push the lid inside the base once more. Keeping the sides of the box in place, bring the bottom flap up along the valley fold and tuck in the side panels against the open end as you did in step 6. Pinch to confirm the corner folds.

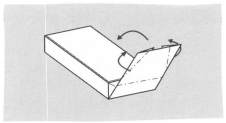

12 Push the bottom flap against the end of the box and fold the tongue over the top of the box to form the horizontal peak fold shown. Taper the corners of the tongue by making the two diagonal peak folds shown; leave a gap of at least 0.5cm (¼in) between the horizontal fold and the start of the diagonal folds.

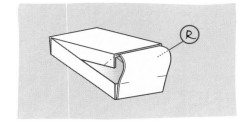

13 Raise the lid of the box and make a diagonal peak fold from the bottom edge of the side panel to halfway up the front edge, then form an inside fold at the corner. Repeat on the other corner.

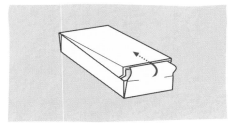

14 To close the box, roll the tongue over and insert the end between the double sheet that forms the inside of the lid. Push the tongue fully flush to lock the box shut. Your card box is now complete.

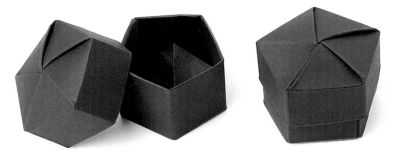

This is a classic and elegant design, its symmetry

and proportions based on principles of geometry.

Once you have mastered the basic construction, you can

PENTAGONAL BOX

make it in

any size.

The lid is made in exactly the same way as the base but has to be fractionally larger in order to fit

on top, so use a slightly larger piece of paper. To make a small box about 6cm (2 in)

in diameter, use a sheet of thick card measuring

19 x 9.5cm (7 1/2 x 3 3/4 in) for the base,

and another sheet about

0.5cm (1/4 in) larger

in both directions

for the lid.

INSTRUCTIONS FOR PENTAGONAL BOX

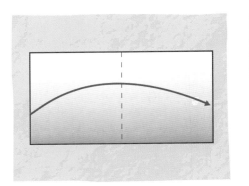

1 Place the card sideways on and valley fold in half from left to right.

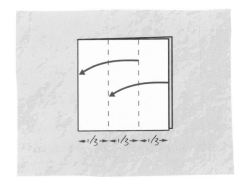

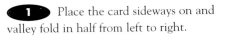

2 Divide the top sheet vertically into thirds by valley folding as shown.

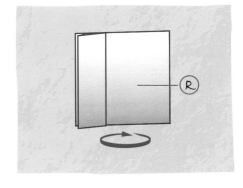

3 Turn the model over and repeat step 2 at the back.

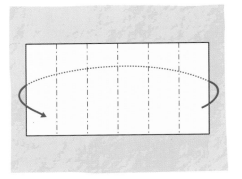

4 Open out the model and define all the fold-lines as peak folds. As you do so ...

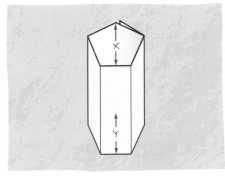

5 ... the model naturally forms the pentagonal shape illustrated. Measure the dimension across the open top of the model (X). Measuring from the base of the model upwards, mark this same dimension on the outer wall of the model (see Y).

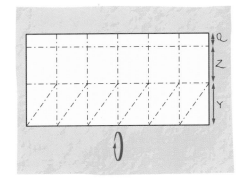

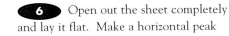

6 Open out the sheet completely and lay it flat. Make a horizontal peak fold across the sheet, using the point you marked at Y in step 5 as the marker to fold from. Dimension Y will form the base of the box. Make another peak fold across the top of the sheet so that dimension Q measures about 0.5cm (¼in). (If you are making a larger box, you should increase this dimension accordingly.) This leaves dimension Z, which will be the height of the box.

Starting from the right-hand bottom edge, peak fold each rectangle of fold-lines in half diagonally from bottom left to top right (making them into triangles), each time pressing the paper flat and unfolding it out again.

Turn the model over in the direction of the arrow so that dimension Q is now at the bottom.

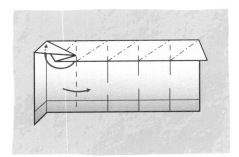

7 Holding the model in the air, valley fold the top section along the existing horizontal fold-line so that, looking at it from above, the diagonal peak fold-lines in each rectangle run from top right to bottom left. Pinch the paper at the top lefthand corner and gently push to the right so that the peak fold moves across and closes up over the adjacent rectangle, as shown in the diagram.

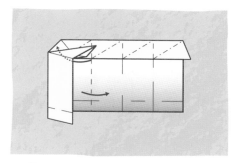

8 Continue folding the diagonal peak folds under each other another four times, keeping them pressed together between your thumb and finger. As you fold the sheet it will curl round to form ...

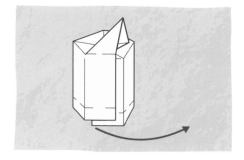

9 ... the shape shown here. In the next step the two end panels, which lie left over right, are to be reversed right over left and the flap sticking up at the top is to be tucked inside to close up the box. First, pull out the end panel underneath in the direction of the arrow.

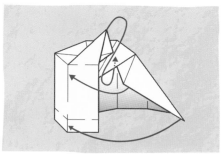

10 Hold the model with two hands, both thumbs inside it and forefingers on the top. Holding the end flaps apart with

your thumbs, use your left forefinger to push firmly the loose flap at the top underneath the flap at the point of the arrow, following the direction of the arrow. Now push the end flaps back together, sliding the right one over the left.

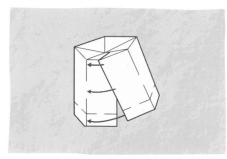

11 Complete this manouevre by firmly pushing the right flap over the left until they lie flush.

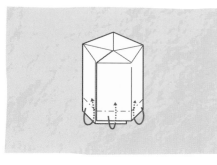

12 Now fold in the peak fold which you made in step 6 to form dimension Q. Start with the double panel and continue around the remaining four panels. This fold gives the top edge of the box extra strength.

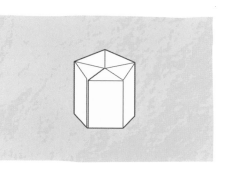

13 You have now completed the base of the pentagonal box. Turn it over and put it aside. To make a lid for the box, repeat steps 1 to 12 with a sheet of card measuring 19.5 x 10cm (7¾ x 4in).

The Pentagonal Box, once mastered, lends itself to many different uses. This handsome pencil case was made using a sheet of paper 25 x 12.5cm (9 ³/4 x 5in) for the base and 12 x 13cm (4 ³/4 x 5¼in) for the lid.

FINAL FOLDS

✳ THIS CHAPTER CONTAINS MORE AMBITIOUS DESIGNS, SHOWING HOW TO MAKE BEAUTIFUL DECORATIVE MODELS AS WELL AS THE MORE FUNCTIONAL OBJECTS SHOWN PREVIOUSLY. ✳ ALTHOUGH THESE MODELS, INCLUDING THE TREE FROG AND STUNNING SUN AND MOON DESIGNS, ARE MORE COMPLEX, THEY USE THE SAME TECHNIQUES WITH WHICH YOU SHOULD NOW BE FAMILIAR. ✳ WITH PRACTICE AND PATIENCE, YOUR RESULTS WILL BE A LASTING REMINDER OF THE INFINITE POSSIBILITIES OF ORIGAMI. ✳

CRANES IN FLIGHT

The delicate beauty of the crane is captured so effectively in this origami representation. It looks intricate, but in fact the method is quite straightforward. Once you have mastered the crane base, you should proceed easily.

I had the idea of making a series of crane models to give the impression of a crane in flight, rather like the frozen frames of an animated film. I made several cranes all exactly the same, but then by adjusting the angles of each one's legs, neck and wings with gentle bending, I created a sequence of movements illustrating how the bird takes off. To get this effect you need to mount the models in a line, and instructions on how to do this are given in the caption. These models were made using a square of fine white paper about 10 x 10cm (4 x 4in); this produces models about 5cm (2in) high. You will find it easier to practise with a larger square until you feel more confident.

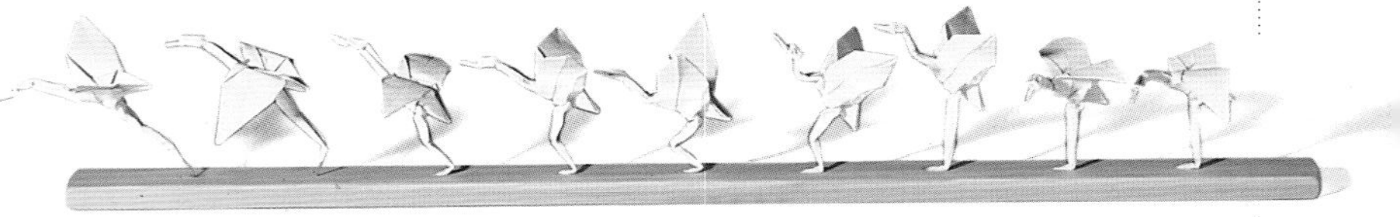

Above *To mount your models on wood as shown here, simply make holes at regular intervals in a block using a bradawl. The final few holes should be progressively more angled so that the crane, once mounted, appears to be taking off. Glue one end of a short piece of thin wire into each hole then glue the other end to the crane's leg. Bend the wires to create a realistic flight sequence.*

INSTRUCTIONS FOR CRANES IN FLIGHT

First complete the Crane Base (page 38), ensuring that the flaps with a concealed triangle in between are uppermost.

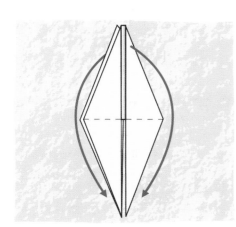

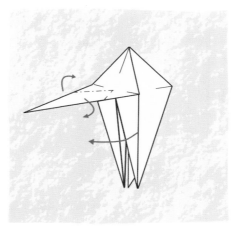

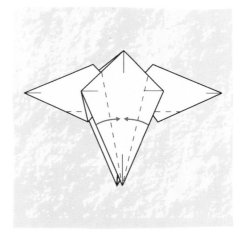

1 Valley fold the upper section down over the lower section (top layer only), folding along the existing horizontal fold-line. Repeat at the back, creating the 'kite' shape shown in diagram 2.

3 Hold the flap between finger and thumb and rotate it 90° in the direction of the arrows. As you do so the front section of the flap will fold back over the wing (see diagram 4). Press flat to create the peak and valley folds shown at the base of the wing.

5 Valley fold the left and right edges of the body in to meet the centre fold-line. As you do so, the wings will lift and you will see two raised triangular flaps at the inner base of each wing; valley fold and press these flat to create the shape shown in diagram 6.

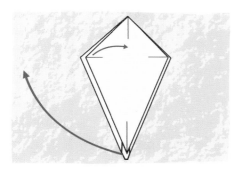

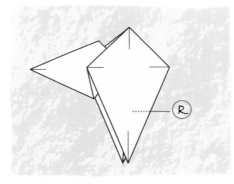

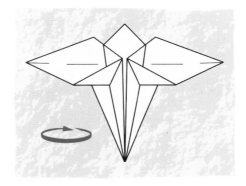

2 To make the wings, raise the left-hand flap to a 90° angle to allow you to lift up the large pointed inner flap to the angle shown in diagram 3.

4 The model should now look like this. Repeat step 3 on the right-hand flap to create the other wing.

6 This is how the model should look. Now turn it over.

INSTRUCTIONS FOR CRANES IN FLIGHT

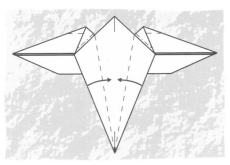

7 Repeat step 5. This time, as you fold in to the centre the raised triangular flaps form at the inner tops of the wings. Valley fold and press flat as before.

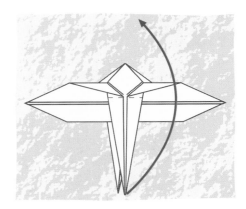

8 Lift the pointed flap (top layer only) and valley fold it back completely, folding along the existing fold-line.

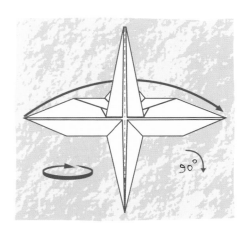

9 Peak fold the model in half from left to right along the vertical fold-line,

then rotate it through 90° so that the wings are uppermost. Now turn the model over in the direction of the arrow.

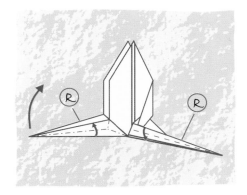

10 The model looks like this; the left-hand pointed section will form the neck, and the right-hand pointed section the legs. Starting with the uppermost leg, valley fold the top edge down to meet the bottom edge. Press flat. Repeat at the back. This makes the legs thinner and more elegant. Make the neck thinner by peak folding in at the front and back, as shown. Push the neck up in the direction of the arrow until the base butts up against the edge of the wings.

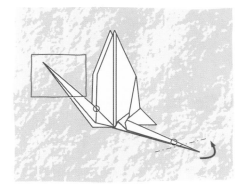

11 Pinch firmly where indicated to confirm the folds formed at the base of the neck. Now suggest the crane's feet: pinch the legs together, a little way in from the end, and lift up the point slightly. Make a peak fold as shown.

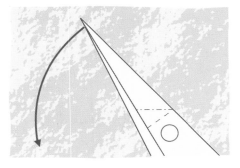

12 To form the crane's head, make a crimp fold. Pinch the neck a little way in from the end and make the peak and valley folds shown in one movement by bringing the point down in the direction of the arrow and pinching into place the folds which naturally form.

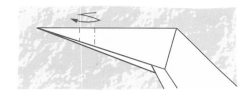

13 Suggest the beak by making a pleat fold close to the point of the head.

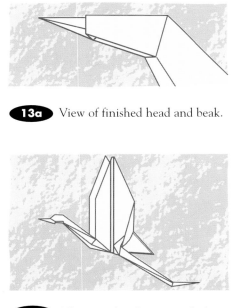

13a View of finished head and beak.

14 The completed crane in flight.

Seahorses are extraordinary and appealing creatures with their elegant equine profiles and uncanny ability to swim along upright. You can make this model in any size you like: large models make decorative

SEAHORSE

sculptures and small ones can be made into items of

jewellery such as brooches or earrings.

To practise, start with a fairly large square sheet of paper, as it is harder to make a tiny model neatly. A square sheet measuring 38 x 38cm (15 x 15in) will give a model about 23cm (9in) long from head to tail. Start with the Seal Base before completing the simple Seahorse steps.

I prepared the paper in advance by spattering blue paper with iridescent

speckles so that the finished

model has a sparkly surface.

INSTRUCTIONS FOR SEAL BASE

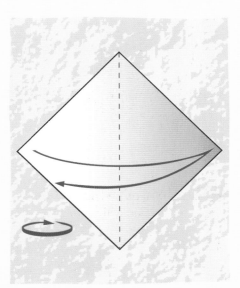

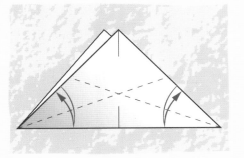

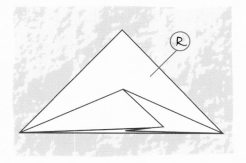

1 Turn the sheet around to form a square diamond shape. Valley fold from left to right. Open out the sheet again and turn it over.

3 (Top sheet only) valley fold the left-hand sloping edge down to align with the bottom edge. Press flat and open out. Repeat on the right-hand side.

6 Turn the model over and repeat steps 3-5, this time folding the 'rudder' to the left.

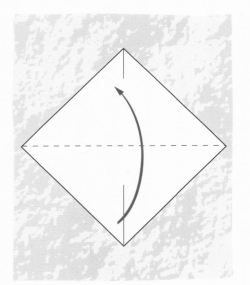

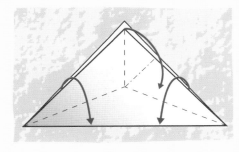

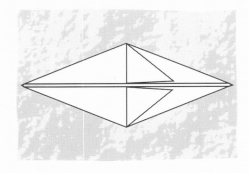

4 Valley fold the top sheet along the existing fold-lines, running your fingers from the bottom corners to the point where the fold-lines intersect. As you do so the top triangle naturally moves down and closes to form a 'rudder' shape. Refer to diagram 5 to see the resulting shape.

7 Pull the back sheet down in the direction of the arrow, opening out the model to form ...

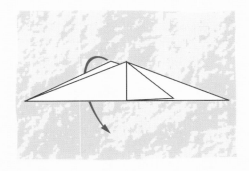

2 Valley fold the sheet in half from bottom to top to form a triangle.

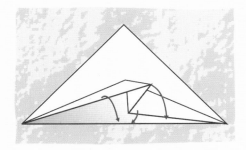

8 ... the completed seal base.

5 As you fold the flap down, make the diagonal peak fold shown in diagram 4 to confirm the 'rudder' shape.

INSTRUCTIONS FOR SEAHORSE

Having completed the Seal Base, continue making the seahorse as shown below.

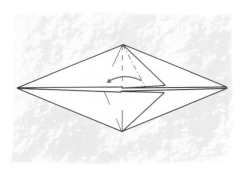

1 Raise the top triangular flap up along the vertical fold-line to a 90° angle. Open out the flap and flatten it to make the shape shown in diagram 2.

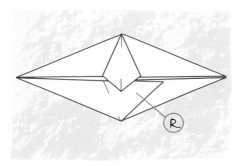

2 Repeat for the bottom flap, flattening it so that it lies over the top flap.

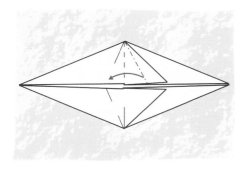

3 Turn the model over.

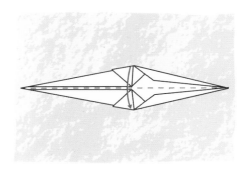

4 Make the two valley folds indicated above, so that the sloping edges meet the centre fold-line.

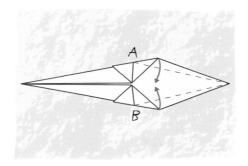

5 Now make the two valley folds shown – these will not meet in the middle. Ensure the folds start from points A and B.

The finished seahorses are shown transformed into attractive and original earrings. This is quite easy to do; all the equipment and information you will need is readily available in most craft or bead shops. Fittings are available for both pierced and unpierced ears.

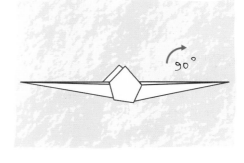

6 Now valley fold the model in half in the direction of the arrow.

7 Rotate the model 90° in the direction of the arrow to the position shown.

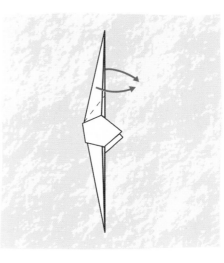

8 Make an outside fold in the top part of the model to make the shape shown at the next step. It may help you if you first define the valley fold-line shown.

INSTRUCTIONS FOR SEAHORSE

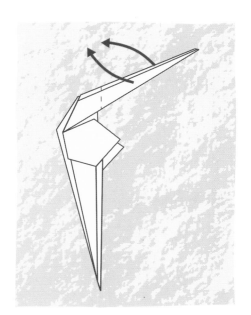

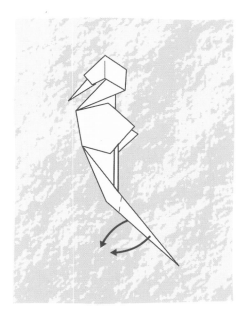

9 Now make an outside fold in the top section to make the shape shown in the next step. It may also help to open out the top section while you do this.

11 Complete the zig-zag fold shown above to make the seahorse's nose.

13 The next five steps create the distinctive curly tail. Make an outside fold along the line shown above.

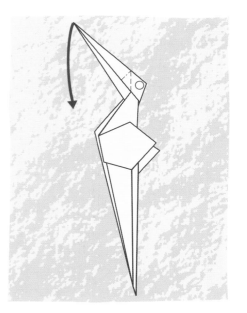

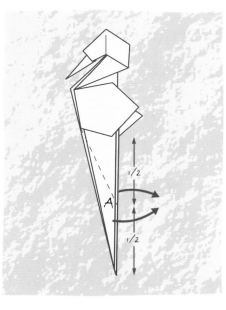

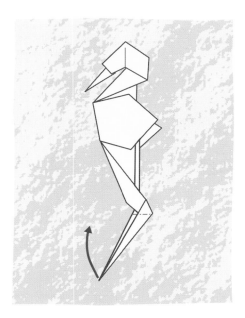

10 Pinch the head of the model. Make a crimp fold by bringing down the nose in the direction of the arrow and pinching together the folds that you have created by this movement.

12 Estimate the centre point of the tail, shown as A above. Make an outside fold starting at this point. As before, you can define the valley folds on either side first if you find it helpful.

14 Now make an inside fold in the tail in the direction of the arrow.

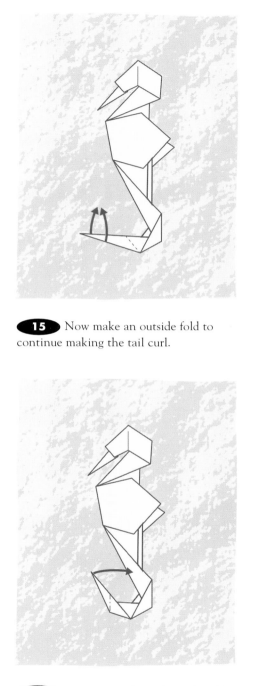

15 Now make an outside fold to continue making the tail curl.

16 Continue making the tail curl by making another inside fold.

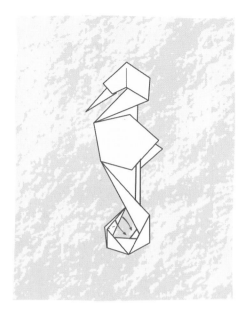

17 The final curl in the tail is made by making an inside fold in the tip.

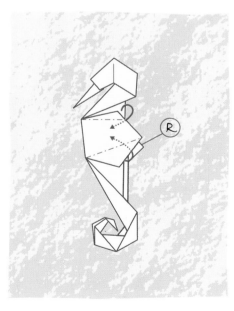

18 Make two peak folds as shown and tuck them behind the wing in the direction of the arrows. Now repeat this movement on the other wing.

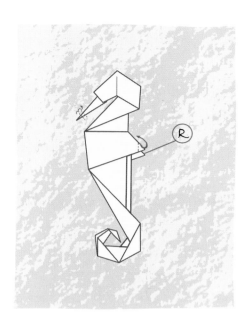

19 Round off the wing tip by making a little peak fold as shown. Repeat on the other wing. To make the final adjustment to the nose, make a small zig-zag fold right at the tip as shown.

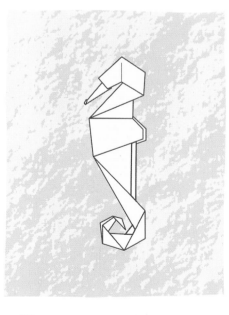
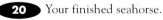

20 Your finished seahorse.

The use of angular folds in this project and the way the tail is bent slightly sideways give a life-like look to the model shark and suggest the way the body swishes as it streaks through the water.

SHARK

Use a silvery, metallic-coated paper to capture the shark's sinister gleam, or decorate your own paper with silver paint speckled with blue and green. Alternatively, you could paint or spray the finished model. A group of circling sharks would make a good mobile.

Use a 21 x 21cm (8 x 8in) square sheet of paper while you are learning, to produce a model around 15cm (6in) long.

84

INSTRUCTIONS FOR FOUR-CORNER BASE

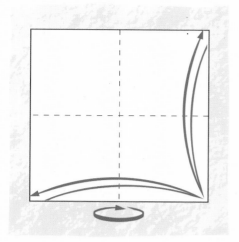

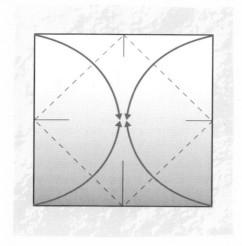

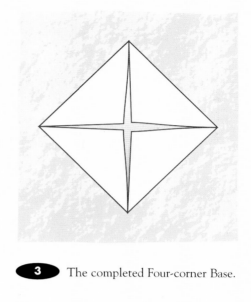

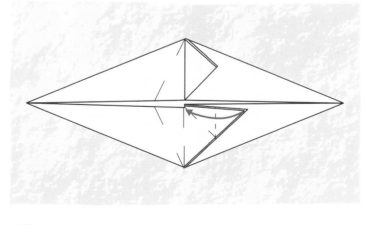

1 Valley fold and open out the square in half from top to bottom then from side to side. The vertical and horizontal fold-lines intersect at the centre of the square. Turn the sheet over.

2 One by one, valley fold each of the four corners in to the centre.

3 The completed Four-corner Base.

INSTRUCTIONS FOR SHARK

After completing the Four-corner Base, make a Seal Base following instructions on page 82. It is important that you start the Seal Base with the Four-corner Base face-up, in the position shown at step 3 above. To check that your Seal Base has been completed correctly, refer to the diagram of the Seal Base on page 90 at the beginning of the dolphin project.

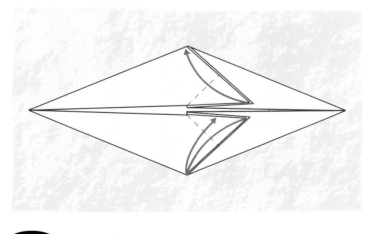

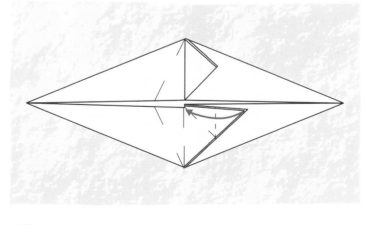

1 Make a valley fold in each triangular flap as shown. Leave the top flap folded, and unfold the lower flap.

2 Make a valley fold in the lower flap as shown.

INSTRUCTIONS FOR SHARK

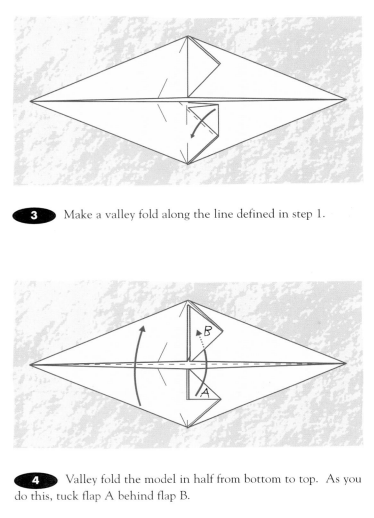

3 Make a valley fold along the line defined in step 1.

4 Valley fold the model in half from bottom to top. As you do this, tuck flap A behind flap B.

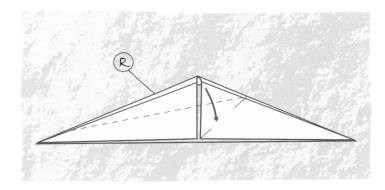

5 Fold down the top flap as shown so that the right edge aligns with the diagonal fold underneath. Turn the model over and repeat the fold on the other side.

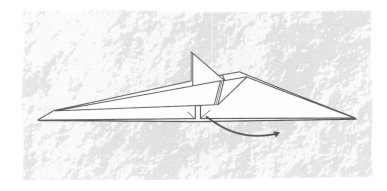

6 Turn the model back over and pull out the single layer of paper indicated by the arrow in the direction shown. Press it flat into the position shown in step 7.

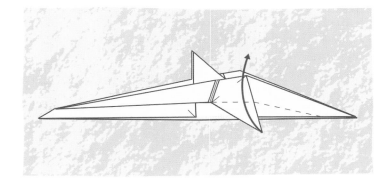

7 Lift up the flap in the direction shown and flatten and define the valley folds created by this movement.

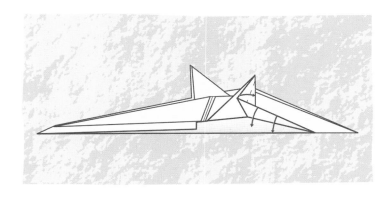

8 Reshape the fold by sliding your index finger into the pocket of the fold you have just flattened and pulling down the lower flap. Press the newly formed vertical flap flat, as shown in the next diagram.

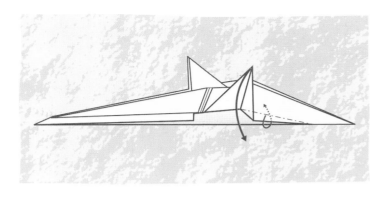

9 Peak fold the edge of the lower right-hand flap by tucking it underneath itself in the direction of the small arrow. Now bring down the top flap in the direction of the larger arrow.

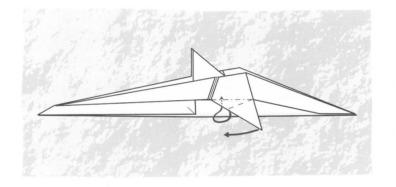

10 This flap represents a fin. Make it more realistic by making a valley fold under the peak fold as shown to create the shape shown at step 11. Repeat at the back.

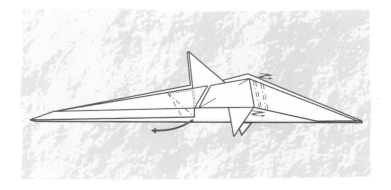

11 To make the gills, make two zig-zag folds as shown, parallel to the line of the fin. Now pull out the corner in the direction of the arrow to create the shape shown in step 12. Define the peak and valley folds thus formed. Repeat both movements at the back.

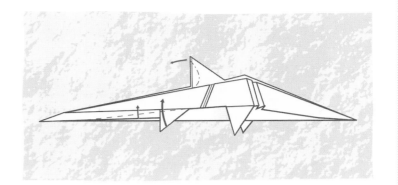

12 Make small peak folds at the back and front of the top fin to make it appear curved and more life-like. Pull the tip down slightly. Valley fold up the underside as shown. Repeat at the back.

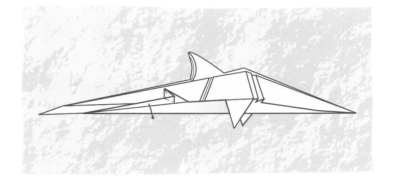

13 Slide your index finger into the pocket made in the last step. Pull down the flap and flatten the vertical flap to complete the movement, as you did in step 8. Repeat at the back.

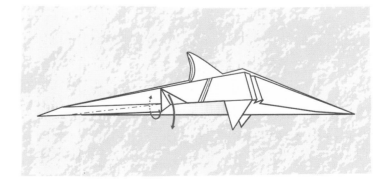

14 Now make a peak fold in the long flap to the left of the lower fin, as shown. This will give the underside a more streamlined appearance.

INSTRUCTIONS FOR SHARK

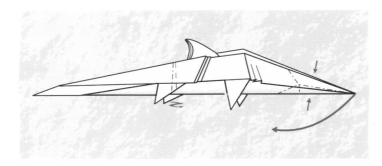

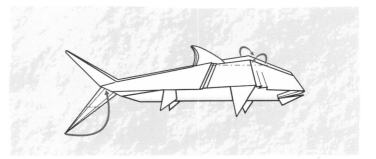

15 Make the back lower fin look more realistic by making a zig-zag fold in its right edge to create the shape shown at step 16. Repeat steps 14 and 15 at the back.

Now create the shark's distinctive nose. Make the peak folds shown by pushing the top and bottom of the nose together in the direction of the arrows at the same time pulling the tip of the nose down, to create the shape shown in the next step.

18 Make an inside fold in the lower tail fin, tucking the pointed end in towards the body. Create a peak fold along the top of the model to make the shark's back flatter. Repeat at the back.

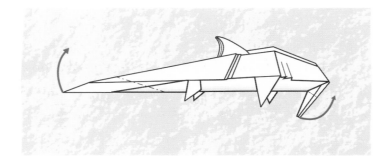

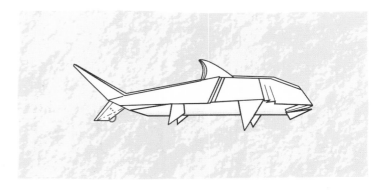

16 Make an outside fold in the tip of the nose and an inside fold in the tail to create the shape shown at the next step.

19 Make another inside fold in the lower tail fin to make the final shape of the tail.

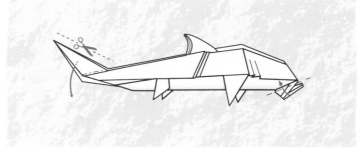

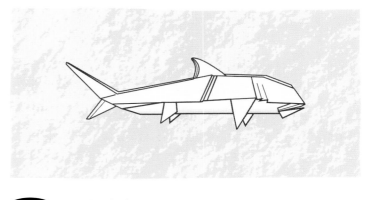

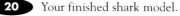

20 Your finished shark model.

17 Valley fold either side of the jaw to make the shape shown in the next diagram. Now take a pair of scissors and cut along the length of the tail as shown. Peak fold down the nearside part of the tail to create the shape shown in the next diagram.

DOLPHIN

Dolphins are highly intelligent and graceful creatures that have a very special place in our affections. I think this model captures their benign character and the beauty of their motion as they leap in and out of the water.

Use fairly thin paper to make this model to avoid it becoming too bulky and difficult to fold; I suggest a weight of 130gsm. Start with a 21 x 21cm (8 x 8in) square sheet of paper. The dolphin model is very similar to the shark model – you begin in the same way, making the Four-Corner Base, the Seal Base and then completing the first ten steps of the shark design.

Remember that the finishing touches are to round off the sharp edges by moulding the paper with your fingers, emphasizing the smooth streamlining of the dolphin's profile.

INSTRUCTIONS FOR DOLPHIN

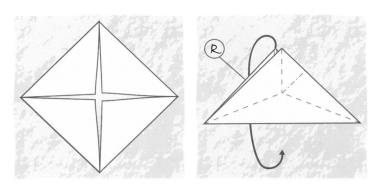

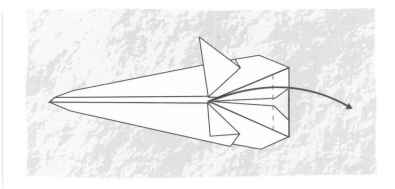

S tart by completing the Four-corner Base (see page 85), Seal Base (see page 80) and steps 1-10 of the shark design. Make sure that you begin folding the Seal Base with the Four-corner base face-up, as shown above.

3 Valley fold this point back out again, folding about two-thirds of the way along the triangular shape.

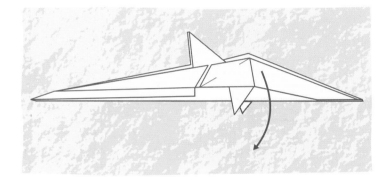

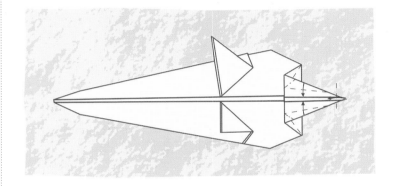

1 Unfold the top flap in the direction of the arrow to make the shape shown in step 2.

4 Now make a valley fold in the top part of the shape you have created, causing the nose shape to taper in. As you do so, the other peak and valley folds shown will form, making a neat flap as shown in step 5. Define these folds, and repeat on the lower part. Make a vertical valley fold right at the tip of the nose shape.

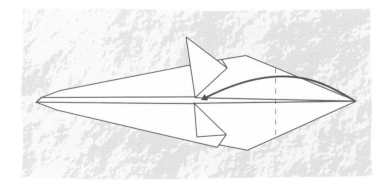

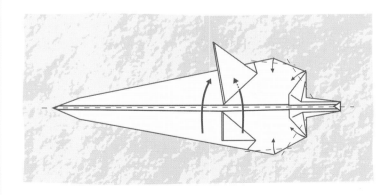

2 Make a vertical valley fold the at the tip of the model to the point indicated by the arrow head.

5 Make the four small valley folds shown, to create the rounded shape of the dolphin's head. Valley fold the model in half, tucking the bottom triangular flap under the top one as you do.

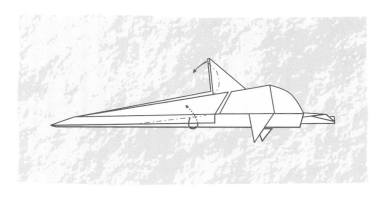

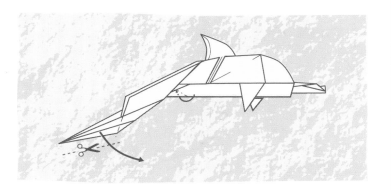

6 First make the top fin more realistic by making peak folds at front and back of the fin, pushing gently on the top of the fin in the direction shown. Now make a peak fold in the lower part of the model, tucking it back underneath itself. Repeat at the back.

9 Make the small diagonal peak fold shown on the underside of the dolphin, to make his shape sleeker. Repeat at the back. Then take scissors and cut along the centre of line of the tail. Valley fold down both sections of the tail.

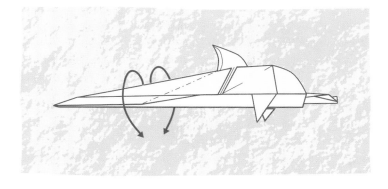

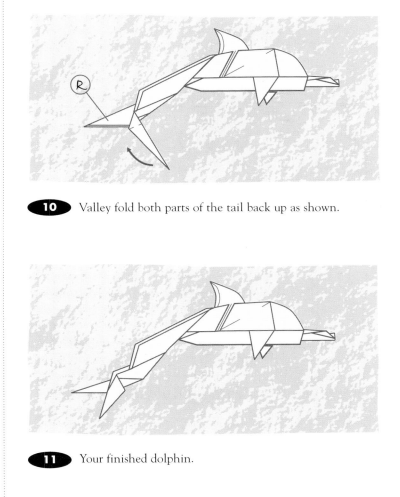

7 Make a peak fold down along the dolphin's flank as shown. Repeat at the back.

10 Valley fold both parts of the tail back up as shown.

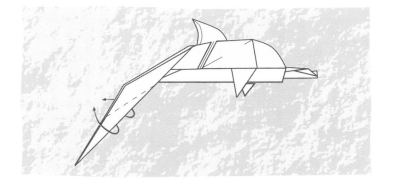

8 Make diagonal valley folds on both sides of the tail.

11 Your finished dolphin.

SUN AND
MOON

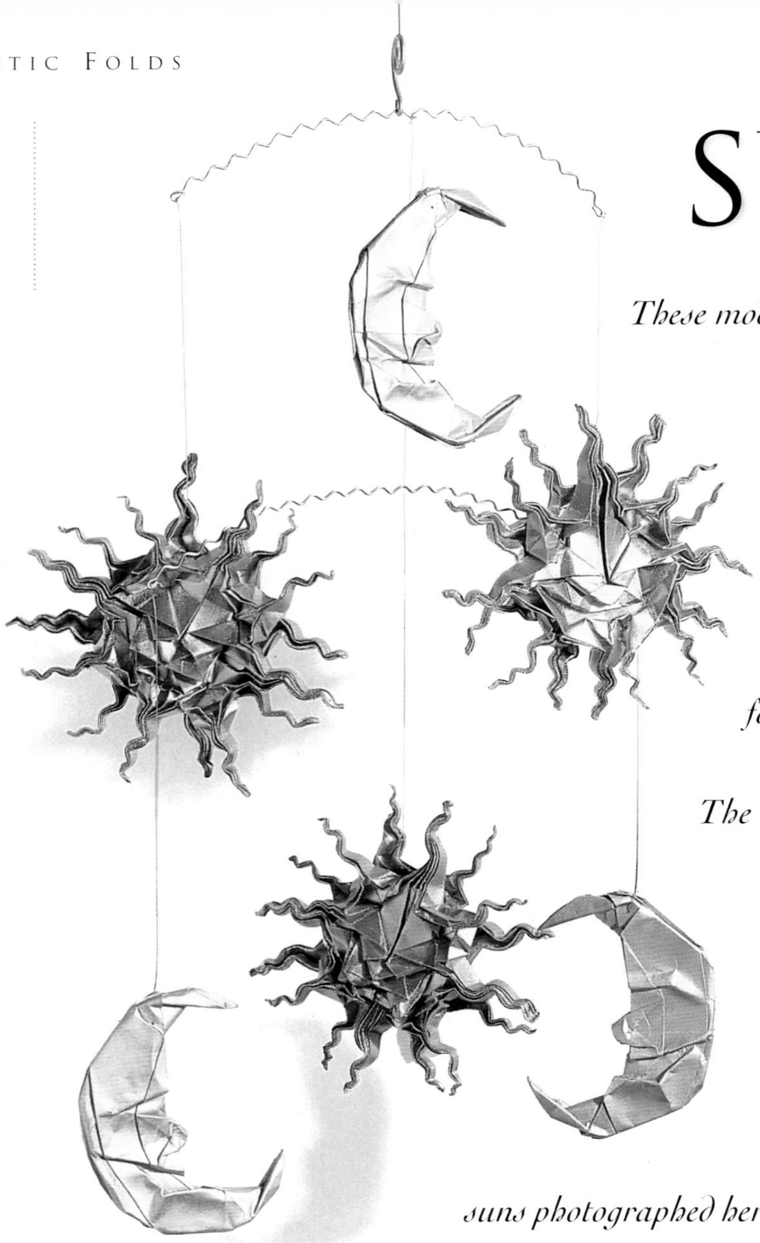

These models look stunning

when put together

to make a mobile. The moon takes a little bit of moulding

at the end; this will be easier if you have practised crimp

folding (see Basic Folds, page 12) before beginning.

The sun is more complex, but will be

straightforward after you have

tackled other projects in the

book. The sixteen-pointed

suns photographed here are made by

simply sticking two eight-pointed

suns together back to back. Complete the effect by

spraying the models with gold and silver paint.

Both designs shown here were made

with a 21cm (8in) square sheet of paper.

INSTRUCTIONS FOR MOON

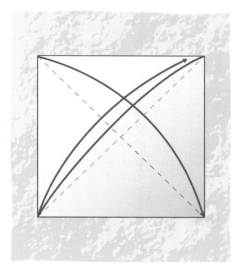

1 Take a square sheet of paper. Valley fold it from the top right to bottom left corner. Press flat and unfold. Now valley fold from top left to bottom right to make a triangle.

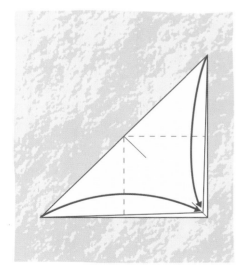

2 Valley fold the top point of the triangle down to the bottom right corner. Valley fold the point at the bottom left corner of the triangle to the bottom right corner, forming a square as illustrated in the next diagram.

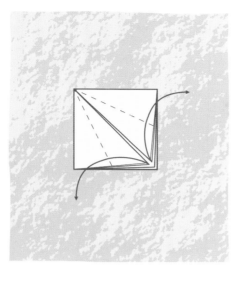

3 Valley fold in the two sides of the square in the direction of the arrows so that they meet at the diagonal line in the middle of the square. Press flat and unfold. Now begin unfolding the model from the tips of the triangles to take you to step 4...

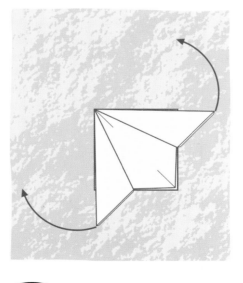

4 ...and continue to unfold the model until you have created the shape shown in step 5.

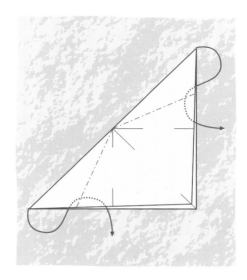

5 Redefine the existing fold-lines as peak folds. Then make inside folds at each of the two corners.

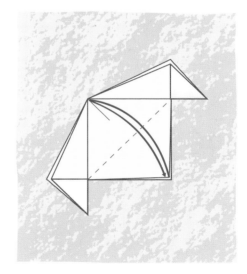

6 Valley fold the top sheet in half as shown. Press flat and unfold to create a diagonal fold-line.

INSTRUCTIONS FOR MOON

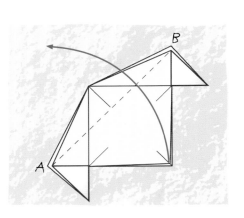

7 Valley fold the top sheet in the direction of the arrow, folding along line AB.

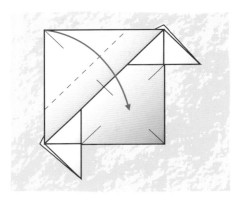

8 Now valley fold the top sheet back in the direction of the arrow along the fold-line you made in step 6.

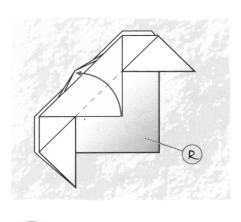

9 Valley fold the top sheet back again in the direction of the arrow. This

side of the model should look as in step 10. Turn the model over and repeat steps 6-9.

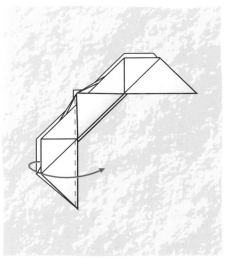

10 Valley fold the bottom section of the model in the direction of the arrow, creating the upside-down kite shape shown in the next diagram.

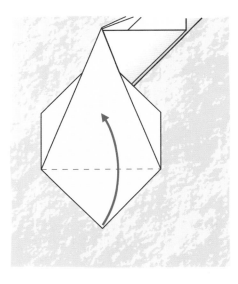

11 Now valley fold the point upwards as shown.

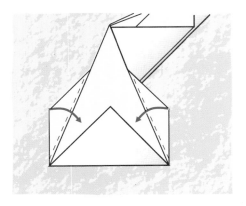

12 Valley fold in the two outer flaps in the direction of the arrows.

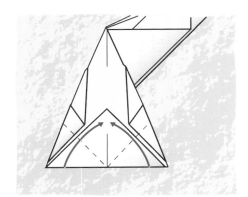

13 Valley fold in the two bottom corners to meet along the centre fold-line.

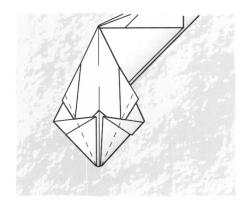

14 Valley fold the corners in again to meet along the centre line.

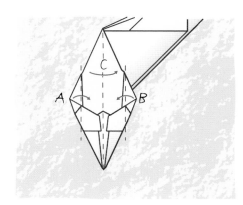

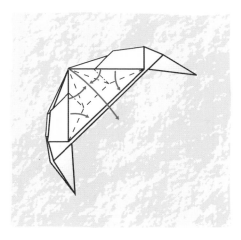

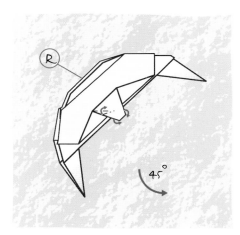

15 This movement is completed in three easy folds. Begin with vertical valley fold A along the fold-line shown, then complete valley fold B. Now valley fold the whole section in half from right to left along line C.

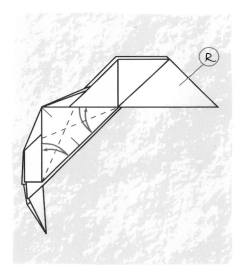

16 Repeat steps 10-15 on the opposite end of the model. Then define the two folds above by valley folding each edge of the triangular flap down to meet the base-line of the triangle. Press each flap flat and unfold.

17 The next movement creates the moon's nose. Begin by valley folding the two sides of the triangle so that their edges meet. Now valley fold the point of the triangle in the direction of the arrow. As you roll the point down, the peak and valley folds shown will form. Flatten the folds to create the shape shown in the next diagram.

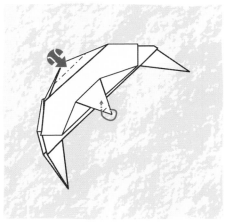

18 Peak fold the point of the nose back and tuck it underneath itself as shown. Now make a sink fold in the spine of the moon to move the point inside the model and make the moon a more authentic crescent shape.

19 To make the nose more realistic, first make two small peak folds in each corner of the nose and tuck them under themselves. Finish off the nose by making a crimp fold as shown to form a nostril. Turn the model over and repeat steps 16-19 at the back.

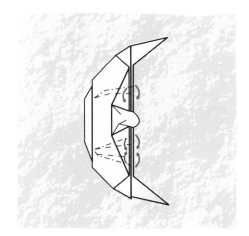

20 Now create the eyebrows and mouth of the moon. Make a crimp fold at the top of the model as shown. This is not an exact fold, and you will need to mould the paper to create the shape you require. Make two more crimp folds to create the mouth, moulding the paper to produce a smile. Repeat at the back.

MOON

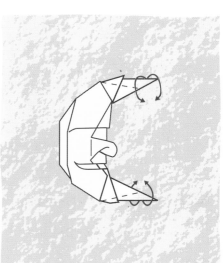

21 Make an outside fold at both pointed ends of the model to complete the crescent shape of the moon.

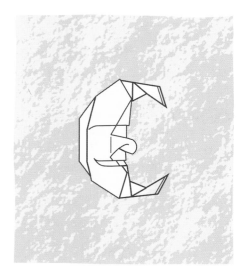

 22 The completed smiling moon.

INSTRUCTIONS FOR SUN

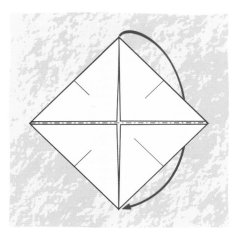

1 Start by making the Four-Corner Base(see page 85). Now peak fold the model in half along the horizontal axis.

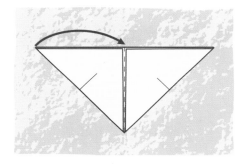

2 Valley fold the model along the vertical axis from left to right and press flat. Lift the top flap to a vertical position.

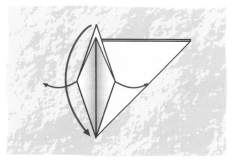

3 Slip one hand into the flap to open it out, then take the top point down to meet the bottom point. Press flat.

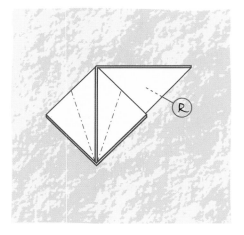

4 Repeat steps 2-3 at the back of the model. Define the two diagonal folds shown on both front and back of the model. Now continue by completing a crane base (see page 38).

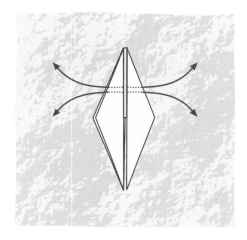

5 With the model in this position, slip your hand into the top left section and pull out the paper from behind the front flap. Repeat on the right-hand side to create the shape shown in step 6. Repeat on the back of the model.

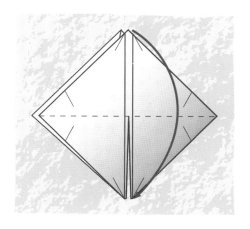

6 Valley fold down the top sheet of the model in the direction of the arrow to create the shape shown in step 7.

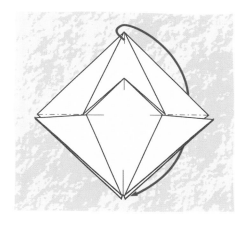

7 Peak fold the model in half in the direction of the arrow.

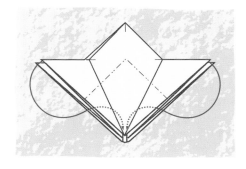

8 Lift the bottom of the front flap and make an inside fold on the right-hand

side of the model, bringing the point down to meet the point at the bottom in the direction of the arrow. Press the fold flat. Now repeat on the left-hand side.

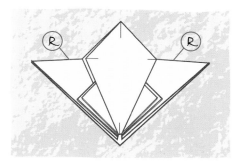

9 Your model should look like this. Turn it over and repeat step 8.

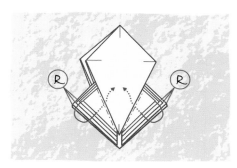

10 Define a peak fold-line on each of the eight flaps. Now make inside folds on each flap, using the fold-lines as guides.

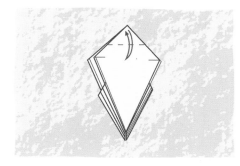

11 Valley fold the point down to the horizontal fold-line, press flat and unfold.

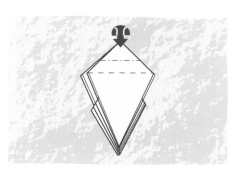

12 Puff the model out with your fingers from underneath. Now open out the square formed at the top in a half-completed sink fold.

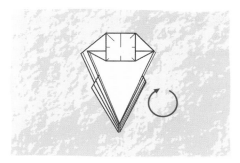

13 Press the square flat as shown. Turn the model over to stand up with all the points in the air. Check that the points of the model are not closed.

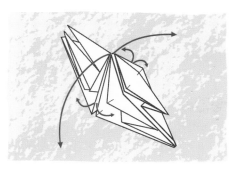

14 Slip two fingers into each side of the model at the base of the small arrows. Then with two other fingers or your thumbs, prise apart the two points indicated at the base of the large arrows.

INSTRUCTIONS FOR SUN

base of each side as shown in step 17. Do this carefully, ensuring that the point is properly symmetrical, otherwise the sun will be lop-sided when completed.

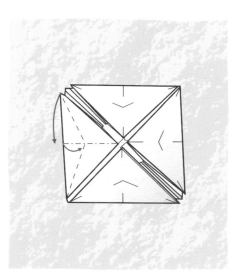

15 Press the model flat in the shape shown. Now lift one of the previously flattened points (shown at the base of the large arrow) so it stands perpendicular to the model. Make sure the inside fold made in step 10 folds back inwards again as indicated by the small arrow.

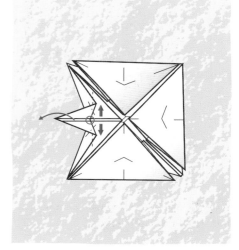

16 Slip one finger into the back of the raised fold to open it out slightly in the direction of the small arrows. Now press down on the pinch point from above with your other hand to flatten the fold out. A small pocket will be created at the

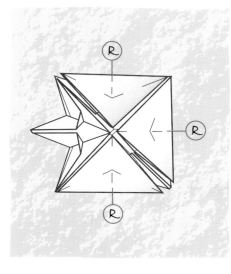

17 Repeat step 16 on the other three sides, trying to make them as even as possible. This will create a total of eight points or radials.

18 Turn the model over and rotate it to the position shown in step 19.

19 Valley fold the central square in half in the direction of the arrow.

20 Valley fold the left edge of the top radial to meet the vertical axis. As you do so the top of the left radial will rise up. Valley fold this down to create the shape shown in step 21. Repeat on the right-hand side of the top radial.

21 Lift up the top of the original central square and peak fold each corner under along the diagonal fold-line.

22 The previous step created the sun's nose. Make the mouth by making diagonal peak folds in the flap underneath the nose. Now valley fold the lower radial along the horizontal foldline, at the same time valley folding in the side edges and the adjoining inside edge of each diagonal radial. Allow the bottom radial to drop back down slightly. Valley fold up the lower edge of each horizontal radial.

23 Now make a pleat fold at the base of the lower radial. Fold in the remaining valley folds on the other radials to create the shape shown in step 24.

24 Press the sides of each radial together (see the arrows) to create a peak fold along the centre of each. Now create a shaped pleat at the base of each radial by pressing down from each side of the fold-lines with your thumbs.

25 Ripple each radial between the fingers of one hand to create the shape indicated by the arrows.

26 Well done! You have now completed the smiling sun.

ELEPHANT

This is an Indian elephant — the African has larger ears! The model is made by modifying the Crane Base to maximize the paper and the various points needed to create the elephant from a single sheet of paper. We used a hand-made batik paper to give our elephant a wonderfully ethnic feel; this paper is quite expensive, though, and you should practise first with some ordinary sheets. Use paper that is not too thick - around 130 gsm would be ideal. To make a model about 15cm (6in) high, you need to start with a sheet of paper about 45cm (17 ³/4in) square.

INSTRUCTIONS FOR ELEPHANT

S tart by completing the Crane Base (page 38). Valley fold down the top flaps to form the kite shape shown below.

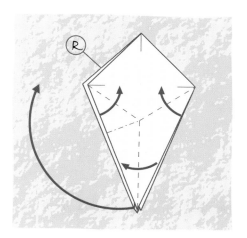

1 Valley fold the left-hand edge of the model to meet the existing horizontal fold-line. Unfold and repeat on the right. Define each fold again – this movement will cause the bottom flap to rise up, and form a 'rudder' shape. This is a similar movement to the Seal Base (page 80). Press the model flat, defining the peak fold and the vertical valley fold shown. Repeat this movement at the back.

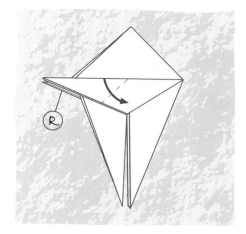

2 Now valley fold the flap formed in step 1 in the direction of the arrow,

bringing the top edge down to meet the vertical crease. Repeat on the reverse side of the model.

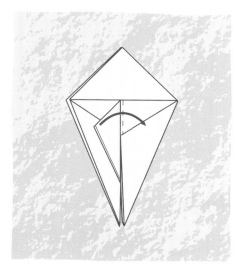

3 Valley fold the flap over in the direction of the arrow and again repeat on the reverse side.

4 Lift up the top flap and pull out the left-hand flap that lies beneath it (from the base of the arrow) to the position shown in step 5. Repeat at the back.

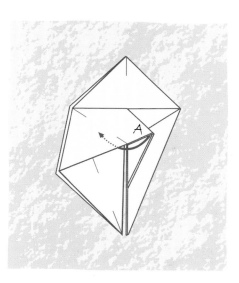

5 Now lift up the top flap at A so that you can unfold the folded flap beneath it in the direction of the arrow. Refer to step 6 for the resulting shape.

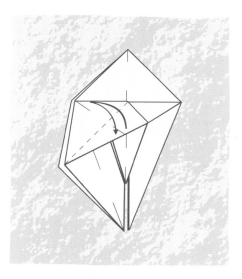

6 Valley fold from the centre to the left-hand point as shown. Press the model flat and unfold.

INSTRUCTIONS FOR ELEPHANT

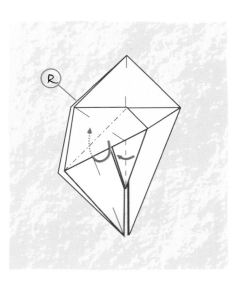

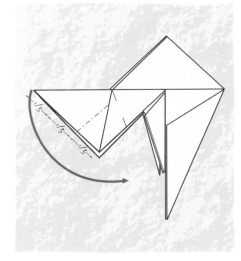

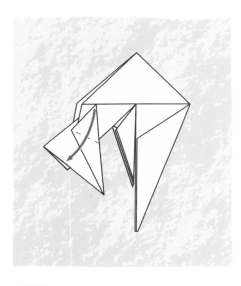

7 Now peak fold along the fold-line you defined in step 6, at the same time valley folding the centre flap from right to left. Repeat steps 5-7 on the back of the model. Diagram 8 shows how the model should now look.

9 Roughly divide the left-hand edge into thirds and complete an inside fold, making the peak fold about two thirds along the flap.

11 Valley fold down the flap in the direction of the arrow.

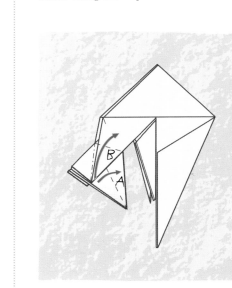

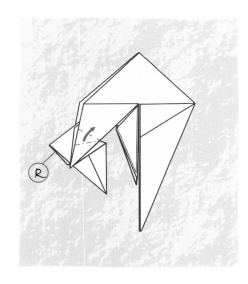

8 Pull out the point of the flap in the direction of the arrow, redefining the existing fold-lines to make the shape shown in the next diagram.

10 Slip your index finger between flaps A and B and make the valley folds shown to create a triangular pocket with a straight vertical edge. Press the folds flat to create the shape shown in step 11.

12 Repeat steps 10-11 at the back of the model. Then make a crimp fold in the top flap by taking the peak fold over the valley fold as shown. Repeat at the back.

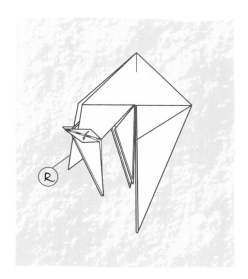

13 Create the tusks by making two peak folds meet along the centre of the top flap, making the shape shown. Valley fold the top flap in half in the direction of the arrow. Repeat at the back.

14 Peak fold the left edge of the 'trunk' to make a more realistic shape. Then make a peak fold in the centre flap which will become the front legs. Repeat both movements on the back. Slip your finger under flap A and pull out the corner from the base of the arrow in the direction shown. Repeat at the back.

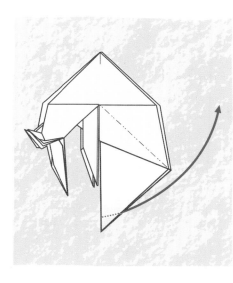

15 Pull up the point in the direction of the arrow, completing an inside fold. This is a similar movement to the one performed in step 8. You may need to open up the model to define the folds.

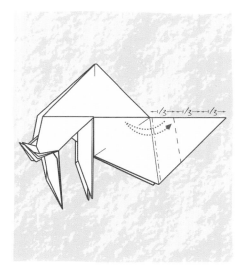

16 Roughly divide the flap into thirds as shown, then perform a zig-zag fold by first making a peak then a valley fold. This forms the elephant's tail.

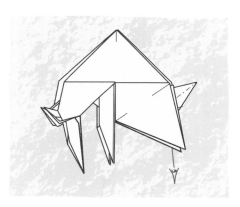

17 Open up the model at the tail end and look at the underside.

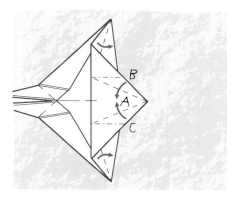

18 This is a close-up of the tail area. Make two valley folds to make points B and C meet at point A. This movement will naturally form the other folds shown.

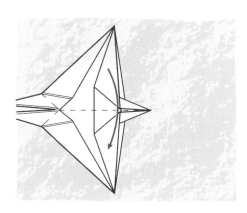

19 Valley fold the model in half.

INSTRUCTIONS FOR ELEPHANT

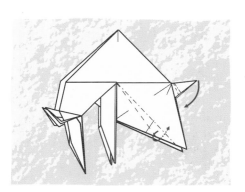

20 Make a crimp fold in the tail in the direction of the arrow. Now crimp fold both back legs, tucking the fold underneath the stomach in the direction shown.

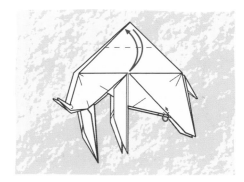

21 Tuck the small peak fold on the underside inside the model. Valley fold the top point down then unfold as shown.

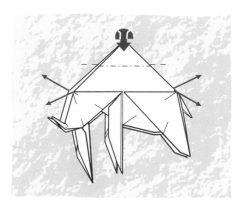

22 Now gently pull out the four corners of the model, as indicated by the

straight arrows. Complete a sink fold at the top of the model using the lines defined in step 21. This will create the elephant's flat back.

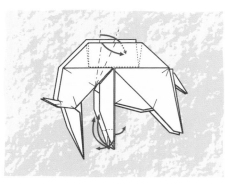

23 Make a crimp fold on either side of the model to create the elephant's ears. Now complete outside folds on both front legs to begin to define the elephant's feet. Lastly, examine the sink fold created at the last step. Push the triangular points out towards the head and tail respectively to create the rectangular shape shown inside the elephant's back.

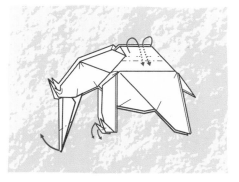

24 Make an inside fold in the trunk of the elephant as shown. Now make outside folds on each of the front feet. Make the elephant's back straighter by peak-folding both sides into the middle of the model along the lines shown.

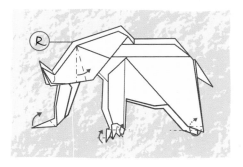

25 Make an outside fold in the trunk. Now firmly crimp fold the head on each side as shown. You will be creating a peak fold along the previous fold-line. Make outside folds on both front feet, then make peak folds in both back feet.

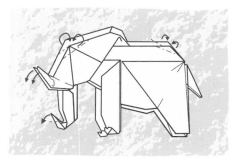

26 Complete the trunk by making a small outside fold in the tip. Pull down the tusks, pressing on either side to define the folds. Round off the forehead and shape the back by tucking the four folds shown inside the model.

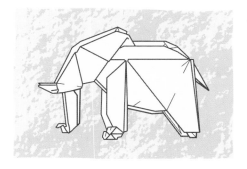

27 The completed Indian elephant.

104

These very lifelike and convincing frogs are accurate models of a type of Panamanian tree frog. Unlike most of the projects in this book, in which decorative papers have been left unadorned, here the finished model is sponge-painted to give it realistic colouring. (To achieve this effect, paint the frog all over and let the model dry. Then simply dip a natural sponge in paint, squeeze out the excess and dab onto your model until you obtain the desired effect.

TREE FROG

When trying this project for the first time, start with a fairly large, square sheet of paper.

A sheet 30 x 30 cm (11¾ x 11¾ in) will fold into a frog about 10 cm (4 in) long and nearly as wide – about a third of the size of your original piece of paper.

Use strong but thin paper for your frog to make folding easier in the later stages.

INSTRUCTIONS FOR TREE FROG TOES

The tree frog is the most intricate project in this book, so to make it easier to follow we have split it into three sections. The first step is to make the toes in each corner of your square of paper. Then make the Frog Base from the square, and finally create the body and angle the legs to produce the finished frog. To make it easier for you to follow the steps, we have not shown the toes on the Frog Base diagrams, except at the first and last steps.

Don't be put off by the long sequence of folds – each step is easy, and you have already learned all the necessary folds.

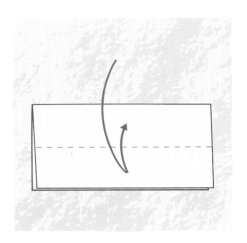

1 Valley fold the paper in half from top to bottom. Valley fold the top sheet in half again from bottom to top.

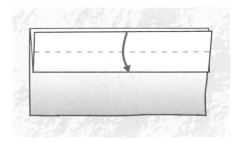

2 Valley fold the top sheet in half to create the shape shown in step 3.

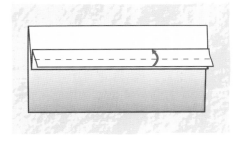

3 Now valley fold up the top sheet for the final time.

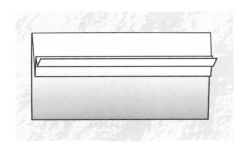

4 Define all the folds and unfold the sheet. Now repeat steps 1-4 on the remaining three sides. Your unfolded sheet of paper should have the fold-lines shown in the next diagram.

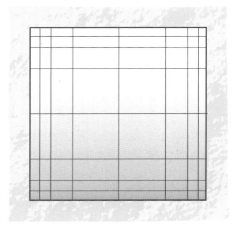

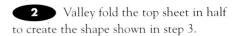
4a Your sheet should look like this.

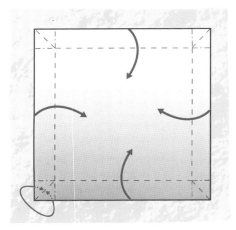

5 Using the second fold-line in from each edge, pinch a corner from underneath to create a diagonal valley fold and bring the adjoining edges in. Press these edges flat along the fold-lines, and press the diagonal fold out to the side to create the shape shown in step 6. Repeat on the other three corners.

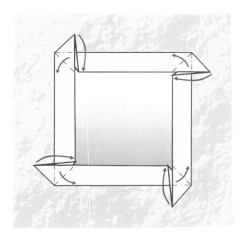

6 Fold each corner flap first one way and then the other to define the diagonal fold-line at its base. Now open it out and press it flat to create a square as shown in step 7.

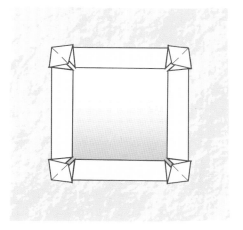

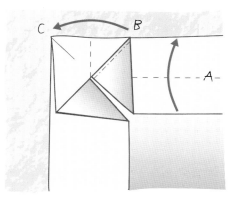

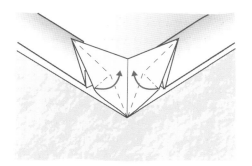

7 Make sure each corner square is symmetrical, then define the folds. These corners will form the frog's toes.

9 Make a valley fold a along the long edge at the top. At the same time, fold point B to meet point C to make a vertical valley fold. Press the paper flat to create the shape shown in step 10.

12 Lift both flaps on one corner of the model to reveal the shape shown above. Valley fold the two flaps in to meet at the centre line and press flat to confirm the folds.

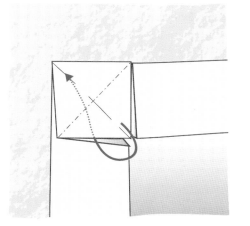

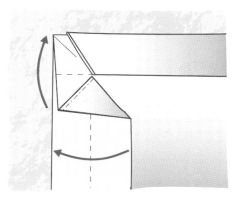

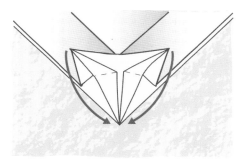

8 Lift the top sheet on one corner flap and peak fold it along the diagonal, tucking the flap neatly inside itself. You may find it easier to make this fold accurate if you fold this as a valley fold first, unfold it and redefine it as a peak fold.

10 Repeat step 9 on the adjoining long edge of the square as shown above..

13 First pinch each top corner then valley fold it down to meet the point at the bottom to complete the fold. Repeat steps 12-13 at each corner.

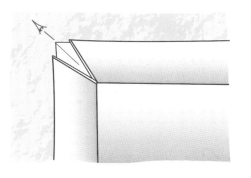

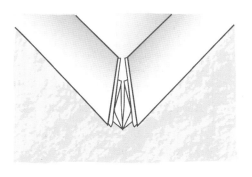

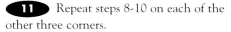

11 Repeat steps 8-10 on each of the other three corners.

14 Each corner should look like this. Now use this sheet to make the Frog Base.

INSTRUCTIONS FOR FROG BASE

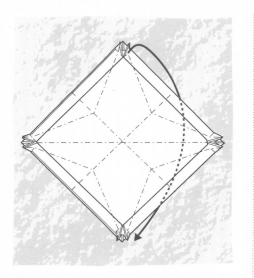

1 It's vital that you start with your paper 'right-side up', like this. With the model in a square diamond position, peak fold it half along the horizontal axis so the toes remain on the outside. Continue to make the Crane Base, following the instructions on page 38.

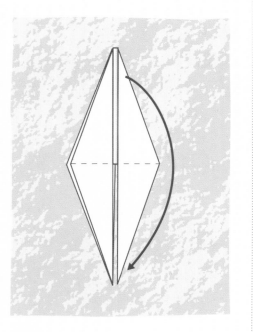

2 Valley fold down the top layer of the Crane Base model along the existing centre fold-line.

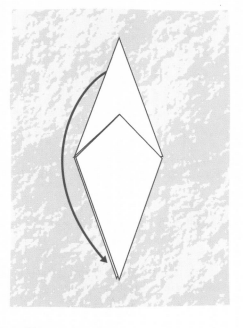

3 Repeat step 2 at the back of the model to create the kite shape shown in the next diagram.

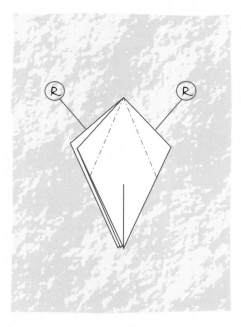

4 Peak fold each of the four flaps as shown, bringing the point to meet at the centre. Press each fold flat and unfold.

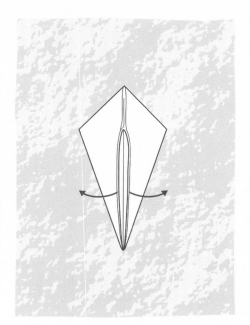

5 Lift up one flap and open out the pocket. Stretch it open, as indicated by the arrows. As you do so, allow the top section of the model to rise up.

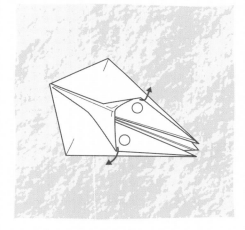

6 Your model should look like this. Continue stretching the pocket open, allowing the top to take on its own shape. The folds you made at step 4 should help you create the correct shape at the top of the pocket.

COMPLETING THE FROG

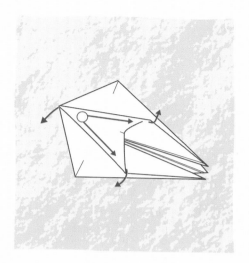

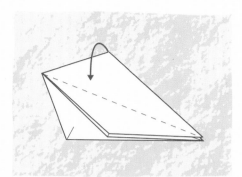

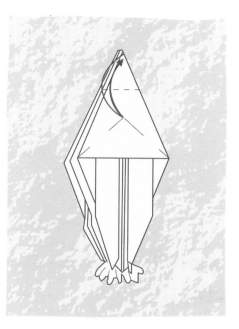

7 Pinch the top of the model and pull it back gently. With your other hand, pull the pocket open as shown, teasing it open with your fingers if necessary.

9 Raise the next pocket to a vertical position, ready to repeat the process.

1 Valley fold down the point of your model along the line as shown so it reaches the top point of the existing fold-lines. Press flat and unfold.

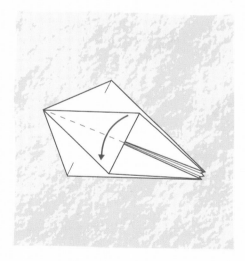

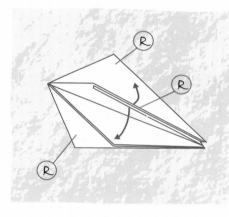

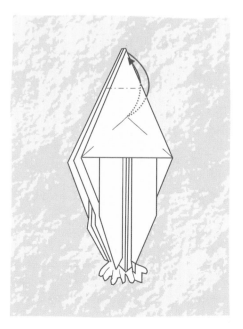

8 Press the pocket flat and define all the folds, keeping it as neat as possible. Now close up the completed section by valley folding it in half as shown.

10 Open out the pocket as before and repeat steps 5-8 on the other three pockets. Try to keep the sections equal, so the frog will have good proportions .

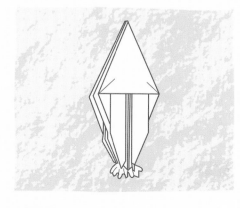

11 Here is the completed frog base.

2 Now redefine this valley fold as a peak fold, by folding it back the other way. As before, press flat and unfold.

COMPLETING THE FROG

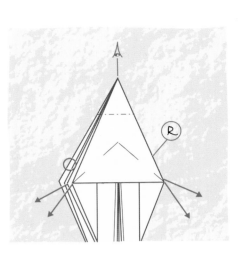

3 Steps 3-4 explain how to make an adjusted sink fold. Start by pulling out the four corners in the direction of the arrows, pinching the two back layers together on each side as shown in step 4.

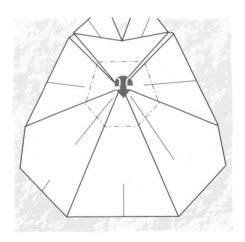

4 This is a bird's eye view of the top of the model. Sink in the top of the model along the fold-lines you made in steps 1 and 2, making sure that you don't open out the two back pleats made in the last step. This movement and the next three steps will create the frog's head and eyes.

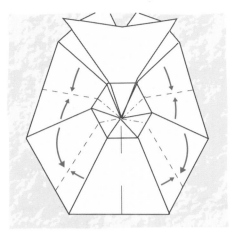

5 Your model should look like this. Now valley fold the four side panels to create the shape shown in step 6.

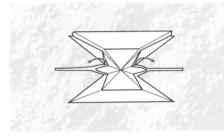

6 Without releasing the paper in each back corner pleat, fold down the two back side sections to create the mouth – you can see this fold most clearly at step 8.

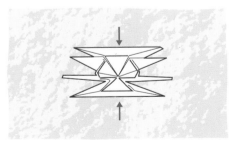

7 Flatten the model to complete the adjusted sink fold.

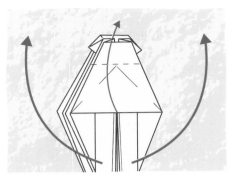

8 Valley fold up the top flap along the fold-line shown, at the same time...

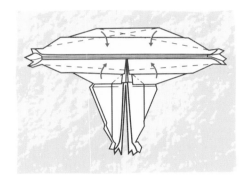

9 ...opening out the two front legs to make this shape. At the top make two intersecting valley folds as shown. Repeat on the lower half of the front legs. As you do so, small pockets will appear in the middle, as shown in step 10.

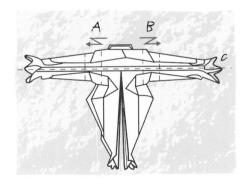

10 Make the pleat folds A and B at the shoulders, folding in the direction of the arrows. Keep these close to the head or the frog will end up with shoulder pads! Now valley fold the arms in half along the horizontal axis.

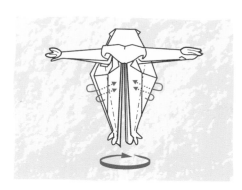

11 From here on the work is easy. Peak fold the top layer of each back leg along the fold-line shown. Turn the model over and repeat on the other side.

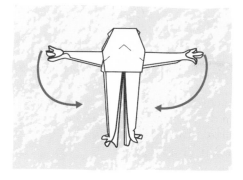

12 Grasp one front foot of the frog and pull it down, creating inside folds at the shoulder. Press the folds flat firmly. Repeat on the other front leg.

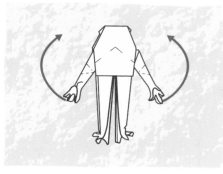

13 Bend the front legs of the frog at the elbow, first defining the peak and valley fold-lines on each one.

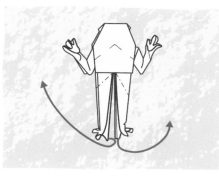

14 Define a peak fold-line on each back leg – note that they should not be symmetrical. Make an inside fold using each fold-line as a guide.

15 Define two more peak folds and make a second inside fold on each leg.

16 Finally, make an inside fold at each ankle along the fold-lines shown.

17 Here is your finished tree frog. If you wish you can make it more realistic by sponge-painting it....

18 or by gluing on a bead for each eye and adding tiny balls of plasticine or similar modelling material to create the pad on each toe.

FURTHER INFORMATION AND SUPPLIERS

If you would like to write to the authors with your comments on the book or if you would like any information regarding FANTASTIC FOLDS' *range of origami services including design, packaging, sculpture, paper jewellery, origami classes and demonstrations, please write to this address, enclosing a stamped, self-addressed envelope:*

FANTASTIC FOLDS
31 St James' Drive London SW17 7RN

If you would like to receive a brochure and information about the FANTASTIC FOLDS *range of solid silver origami jewellery and gifts, send a postal order for £5.00 (refundable against your first purchase) to either of the addresses below:*

Pam Bruton
The Shop on the Bridge
19 Lancaster Place
London WC2E 7EN

Anthea Larr
Combined Harvest
128 Talbot Road
London W11 1JA

PAPER STOCKISTS

UK

Falkiner Fine Papers Ltd
76 Southampton Row,
London WC1B 4AR
Tel: 0171 831 1151

Papeterie Ltd
35 Market Place
Kingston KT1 1JQ
Tel: 0181 546 0313
Mail order service available.

Paperchase
213 Tottenham Court Rd
London W1
Tel: 0171 580 8496
Branches throughout the UK and mail order.

Papyrus
25 Broad Street
Bath BA1 5LW
Tel: 01225 463418

Robert Horne Paper Co.
Huntsman House
Mansion Close
Moulton Park
Northampton
NN3 6LA
Tel: 01604 495333

AUSTRALIA

Handwork supplies
121 Commercial Road
South Yarra
Victoria 3141
Tel: 03820 8399

USA

Aiko's Art Materials Import Inc.
3347 North Clark Street
Chicago
Illinois 60657
Tel: (312) 404 5600

Carriage House Paper
PO Box 197
North Hatfield
MA 01066
Tel: (800) 669 8781

Creative Expression Group inc.
7240 Shadeland Station
Suite 300
Indianapolis
IN 46256
Tel: (800) 428 5017

CANADA

Paper-ya and Kakali Handmade Paper Inc.
9 - 1666 Jonston Street
Granville Island
Vancouver, BC, V6H 352
Tel: (604) 6842531